GILLIAN MK2

GILLIAN FIRTH

Ordering Information:

Prime Seven Media
518 Landmann St.
Tomah City, WI 54660

Printed in the United States of America

TABLE OF CONTENTS

AUTHOR BIOGRAPHY

Well, I turned my computer (toy) on with the intention of doing some work. To write an introduction to let you know who I am, before you 'wade' through this witty masterpiece. But as usual I got momentarily distracted by the card game solitaire. You know the 'I'll do it this time . . . this time . . . this time' Hours later I've either forgotten what was going to be done or I've got to go and do something else. That's who I am.

Anyway, there I was, a young, active, happy go lucky person with a selfish ignorant attitude that comes with youth. I completed my compulsory education and worked in a local supermarket which allowed me to go skiing. Took the option of further education and worked in another supermarket which paid for my driving lessons and helped to pay for another skiing trip. Onto the next stage where my choices were, a crap job that I didn't like, or want, the dole, or university. Easy solution—off I went to Swansea to do a teaching degree. After two years I obtained a diploma and after four years I got my degree. The letters that can be written after my name are DipHE Bed (Hons) phonetically they 'say' that I am dippy in bed! This tickles me but I don't write it and never have, I think it's facetious and who cares.

Whilst doing my student bit I worked in another bar—a superb time— volunteered to work on a kibbutz in Israel, did a parachute jump for charity, had a go at windsurfing, went to beach parties and amongst other things had a full time relationship for five years. He took me to

Paris one Valentine weekend, we went to Spain for a fortnight and so I thought everything was 'happening'. A month before my finals this chap decided to dump me. He turned up on my doorstep one evening with a large bouquet of red roses saying, "Oops, I made a mistake, sorry." He left the next morning and I never saw him again. At the time I was devastated and was crying whilst having a meeting with a very 'proper' tutor, who on pacifying me commented, "All men are bastards." Well it stopped me in my tracks and still makes me smile. I must comment at this point that I had every intention of working in a friends bar in Corfu, when my exams were over and travelling overland back to the UK. To then apply for a job and make use of my newly acquired qualification. Best laid plans of mice and Gill . . .

I did get to Corfu and a few weeks later was sampling hospital food for two weeks. To cut a long story short, I was flown home looking like the elephant man, ultimately resulting in plastic surgery to rebuild my face and about a year getting my life back together. Then off again to Surrey this time, where I had a multitude of jobs that had absolutely nothing to do with my degree—selling insurance, selling wine, cleaning, bar work (again!), working in kitchens, temping, anything but teaching really. This is where I met the man I was going to marry. He was a black belt in karate and was to become my teacher. He called me at work one day, "Good news and bad news . . . good news is I got the job . . . bad news you've got to marry me!" He'd got a job in Saudi Arabia and to continue living together we had to get married to comply with Saudi law. I wouldn't have married had I not wanted to and at the time I had the attitude 'why not'?

This is where I tested my prowess as an educator, finding that I liked it and I was good at it. I joined a band as a backing/lead singer, I liked this too and I thought I was good. Water activities played a large part in my life, I was a keen, if not strong swimmer. My time in this very different country was interesting and another book of tales. Circumstance dictated that we moved to Bahrain, an island just off Saudi. Here I got a good job, made new friends and was enjoying life to the full . . . until . . .

This is a poem I wrote in 1992 for my mum and dad, after I got married and went to live in the Middle East.

MICROSCOPIC VISION

Tiny circular sections magnified, enlarged, refined
We can be blind
It details a world unknown to human eyes
I am just a distant shadow peering in
Probing, prying: to end up crying
Bitter, stinging, burning tears
Through fears I was too close to see
Not with regret but hindsight
Observing a small wonder, not the large miracle
Missing greater events—subtle changes
She was too near, too microscopic
I collected the spangled fair weather laughter
Ignored the rainbow, homing in on the glow of gold
Refused the gift, ravaged the paper
I am so naive so sightless
I cried all the way to flight AF805
I missed you already and you didn't know
Well . . . here goes.

An introduction to all the characters in my book. They are all code named to protect their identities. Though if you knew them, these names would give them away I have no doubt.

SUPPORT WORKERS—all appearing in the 3rd and 4th years.
Spruce Girl—Came to the new flat with me and helped to set it up and start the 'ball rolling'. She has become a friend and is a flamboyant person with character. She bothers to apply full make up everyday, dyes her hair and is aware of, and about, her appearance.

Space Girl—For a brief time worked alongside Spruce Girl. A fun person that made me laugh with a 'grass is greener' attitude. She left and got a sales job—didn't make her fortune and moved on. She has, by all accounts, got a good job in one of the power industries and is happy (for the moment).

Mr Withit—He gave the believable impression that he was 'on the go' and one 'of the lads'. I really liked him too, he was different, he lived on a boat and helped whenever he could. Even if he didn't really know what he was doing.

Mr Efficient—A pleasant chap. I found him mildly irritating, a bit of a 'know all' who always seemed to be trying to 'get the better of me'. Subsequently making me feel stupid, look stupid and pissing me off. Sad thing is, thinking about it, he always thought that what he was doing and saying were the right things for my benefit.

Mr Ego—The name says it all really I don't need to say anything else. God's gift springs to mind—or rather sprang to his. He once said, to myself and another client, he didn't care what we did, "As long as you don't make me look stupid." Well, what can you say? Despite the ego difficulties he was alright. But not that much.

Stickler—It was hard to believe that she was younger than me, I think she had a dinosaur head on her shoulders and took the role of support worker far too seriously—for me anyway. I'm not saying I didn't like her, but I think we may have come from different planets.

MATES—Most 'friends' that I had—in my previous life—have disappeared into thin air as it were. A quite natural occurrence with age and circumstance—events that you don't expect or want when shit like this happens. But the new chums that have come into my life are special people as they like me as I am now—disability and difficulties being part of the package.

Teeny—A young neighbour that visits regularly—saw her today as it happens—she makes me smile and I have a lot of time for her. She is incredibly level headed and has put me right a few times, seeing beyond my nose and thrashes me at scrabble now.(I taught her everything she knows, let me remind her!)

Gadget Boy—He probably needs the least introduction as he played a large part in my life, pre brain trauma, and stuck around for a long time afterwards. A super chap who played quite a noteworthy role for both me and my parents—he was simply there and bothered. He's quite a bit older than me and the time we spent together before the accident may have made a difference. He's now got a girlfriend and lives in a different country hence the communication has ended. I am fully appreciative of his time and input nevertheless.

Teef Geezer—Mate! he's a cockney that I knew previously. Came back into my life totally distraught and disturbed by the news of my accident. We wrote in years one and two, he visited me at Xmas when I was in the flat—year three. I went down to visit him, when the kidney hassle started, my new crowns on my teeth were in place with a temporary fixative. They were loose and then one morning fell out! I was totally freaked and he commented, that he didn't know what all the fuss was about "loads o' me mates av' got dodgy teef!" hence the name. He's a star.

Editor—A lady I met in Tunisia who stayed in touch for a while. In that time she took my jumbled memories and put them into a readable order and created the solid foundations for my book. An undeniable task, for which I thank her profusely.

Giant Fairy—A man that I knew before, who very briefly came back into my life. He is incredibly tall and I am resisting the urge to be mean about him. We had a good fun friendship before and he let me down. He messed about with me physically and mentally, was unfaithful to his girlfriend and as a result changed his phone number and stopped all contact with me. At the time the total denial was upsetting and confusing. That was then—now "I couldn't give a turquoise toss."

Pathetic—So named because he is. He was my husband, we had a pretty good marriage that was not constricting and was fun. We were still in the 'honeymoon' period when this happened. We both had good jobs, outgoing natures, did things together . . . then when the 'going got tough . . .' he went and got somebody else. I don't really remember him, not that I try, but have absolutely no respect for him AT ALL and dislike him immensely for his trick with the car that my dad's still stuck with.

CHAPTER ONE

I have been thinking about doing this for ages—writing a book and telling it as it is. Thinking about it. "The time for procrastination is over . . ." yeah . . . tomorrow, (this from an ex, Elvis-impersonating, school teacher. You know who you are!). "It's" been three years; I'm in my early, (very early) thirties . . . (At this rate my literary attempt will stay right here).

"It's" been three years since I got squashed, three years since my life changed, TOTALLY. Three years since the existence that I had . . . there it was, gone! I could bore you (what do you mean, I am?) with many euphemisms that say the same thing. I have suffered/am suffering a head injury, a brain trauma (damn I'm doing it again!).

Time means very little to me. That's a bonus—time rarely drags. So if we ever meet, and I am stifling yawns all the time— it's not the head injury, just maybe you're boring me.

It was quite bad basically, bad enough to be totally out cold for six weeks and semi-conscious for another month or so. Anyway, from being in a coma, through often tedious rehabilitation, to being in a wheelchair for a year, wobbling about on crutches then walking sticks (and I still do wobble, but this time no crutches or sticks), to this and now. When out and about there are odd stares, and sometimes hurtful remarks by a few. I have to take them 'in my stride', there really is no other way to cope. I know what's wrong with me. I'd like to see how those that gawp, and comment, would cope if EVERYTHING that they took for granted, ie: walking, swallowing, talking, going for a 'wee', was taken from them.

1

In one fell swoop, with no choice. Get over it and cope! But there are LOADS of people that understand head injuries and the implications, these people will help.

There are people in roles, associated with head injuries, who believe that they are perfect and will not admit that maybe sometimes they are wrong, or they really haven't got a clue what they're talking about. They could be termed as 'power freaks'—it must be gratifying to have control over, and always be correct. There are people that criticise nearly all the time. When I, brain damaged, point this out, 'They' then say something nice/positive, followed by, "So, how ARE you? . . . Oh . . . good." They never seem to wait for an answer.

I'm handling this, right or wrong, the only way I can. I know no other way. We each go through life carrying and battling through our own personal nightmares. These are major deals to us. We sometimes surface in a nice bit, with nice things . . . sometimes we don't. One of the most bloody annoying things is that when almost complete disasters like this happen—there is no-one to blame—it is simply nobody's fault. Yeah . . . shit happens! I've got somebody else's load dumped on my doorstep, if anybody's missing it . . . no? OK . . . nice try!

About my injury. I was in a foreign country, driving alone. I was told that I was hit by a drunk driver who raced the lights. I was also told that I raced the lights. Other information I was given was that the other driver, a woman, was in hospital with a broken leg and that he was driving alone . . . you try and piece this together. It doesn't make sense, but as I can't remember anything for at least six weeks out of my life, I guess I'll never know what really happened on the road that night.

I like the "he was drunk" scenario best some days, usually crap days. Other days, other crap days, 'I was totally inebriated', so I deserve this. I had been drinking, and was driving home, in a country where any drinks are illegal. Sod's law. I had forgotten all about this, or didn't even think about it, I'm British, two drinks are the 'legal' limit! Hello! you weren't in Britain dear,

AND you were drink driving! You took the risk, you're paying the price. Simple. I would be interested to know the percentage of serious head injuries that have directly, or indirectly, been alcohol induced. From the people that I have met, quite a high percentage. It only takes ONE time, pregnancy, AIDS, VD, serious head injury, adultery etc etc. Scary. Well this is NOT fun! I think that the British law should be changed for your safety and other road users. Have a gob full and you're drink driving.

Drafted a letter to the transport Member of Parliament, concerning my thoughts on this issue:

Dear Sirs,

I write, still baffled. My local Member of Parliament is in America so spoke to his 'constituency secretarial manager', an aspiring young politician who couldn't commit himself to answer and suggested that I wrote direct to the minister, 'Cut out the middle man' as it were.

Our 'new' government eager to make a powerful gesture to the general public, changed the drink driving laws. General consensus being a calculated 'here here', about time! This is where dodgy grey areas start to appear.

1. Why not a 'have a mouthful and you're drink driving' policy? This would eliminate any confusion. The 'I had a large lunch, I drank ages ago, drinking doesn't affect me, I drive better when I've had a drink' scenarios. Making it clearer for the police too.

2. Do you know the percentage of disabling, sometimes fatal, injuries that are somehow indebted to drink driving? Then you have National Health Service time and costs, including the inevitable rehabilitation which is often years and is extremely expensive. Which also causes unnecessary strains on the already stretched purse strings of the National Health Service. So what are you doing?

It is my opinion that you have muddied murky waters. I'm disappointed. If you're going to do it, do it right! Non of this 'wishy washy' spineless, "well alright you can have one!" it's inconclusive. If you conducted a survey I think you would find we, the general census, reserve this judgement. Or is it, one is limited to a single drink on one's company expenses eh?

Please enlighten me.

Mr Withit (one of my support workers), agreed and added that alcohol free drinks should be cheaper, explaining that at his local one pint of bitter costs one pound fifty pence and half a pint of alcohol free lager is one pound and five pence (a pint would be two pounds and ten pence). Some places even charge for water. Shouldn't drink driving be discouraged? Would incentives to the brewers make it more worthwhile? I'll be OK to drive now . . . only one! It's bullshit! Can you say the same after you've had five? So having one is the lead up, what? the first two or three don't affect you? No, the effects of the alcohol aren't always NOTICEABLE. You don't have to be ruining your street cred, speaking rainbows, to be 'under the influence'. It'll never happen to you?

That must have been my last 'whole' thought.

A 'big and clever' head injury can happen to anybody, anytime. I was found. (My 'editor' asks, "by whom?" Answer is, "I don't know."). The only form of identification I had on me was a business card, given to me by someone I had met that night. My only lucky break. He was telephoned, thankfully, he knew my husband—to be known in future as "Pathetic"—just so you know who I'm referring to, from hereon. Pathetic, was in a different country; he was faxed at work and flew in. I have since been told that he was dreadfully upset. Knowing how he has treated me since the accident, that is sometimes difficult to believe. He didn't call my parents. He said it was because he didn't want to call the UK, saying, "Gillian's in a coma." even though she was. He wanted to call saying, "Gillian WAS in a coma, but she's alright now." This is almost verbatim what he told me when I asked. This makes sense to me, but it would also have been expensive to telephone England! But I think it would have been crap news either way, at any time.

He rang my parents when I had been unconscious for a week. Well, my mum wasn't very happy that he'd been so thoughtful. She was extremely upset, in fact. God! I married an ass, but, I wouldn't have known what to do, or say, either. But still. So my mum and brother flew in, eventually. Wouldn't you just know it, everybody and anybody wanted to come to THIS country at exactly the time that they did. Resigning her thoughts to alternative travel methods, she got a flight! So the hiking boots and swimming costumes were packed away. It's a long flight—must have been beyond a nightmare.

On one of her visits she was sitting and chatting to me imploring me to 'come back!' and was rewarded to witness the very first time I opened my eyes. Thereby postponing (forever!) the tracheotomy. In a coma, your breathing is done for you with a respirator. If it's breathing for you through your mouth for too long there is a danger that your vocal cords will be irreparably damaged. So the tracheotomy is carried out. A hole is made in your windpipe through which you 'breathe', it by-passes the vocal cords and usually leaves a really ugly scar. I must admit to being ever so (smugly) pleased about this now.

Pathetic wrote me a poem in the get well card that he made me.

Her light was feeble, but growing stronger,
Please don't let it be much longer.
Her eyes are open and comprehending,
That love surrounds her there is no pretending.
Slowly awakening, Oh! what a beauty.
No, not here because of duty,
Here because I love her so,
That lovely woman with so much go.

There's nothing that I can say about what happened, I was just there—in body. I'm quite happy to let my mum argue that I recognised her voice, heard her pain. Pathetic must have been heartbroken, he'd been there for days. Subconsciously, I must have known she was there. My mum! Quite happy because I don't know why I opened my eyes when I did. It was just the time? It didn't happen again for days apparently—but it was the start.

Gadget Boy, the last person that I saw on THE night told me that when he visited, "I would ask you to look at various objects and you would, as though your eyes were controlled elsewhere—by remote control." Gadget Boy wrote me a poem in his get well card that he made for me.

> Your mother's tender caring,
> So gently caressing you,
> She whispers words of love so pure
> My baby please pull through.
> Your eyes they flicker open,
> So confused you gaze around,
> Then away you sink to that distant place
> Where sleepless sleep abounds.

An odd thing happened around this time. Two girls I'd been teaching, wanted to come and see me. They loved me! They were told they couldn't go into intensive care. Children not related to the patient weren't allowed. Well, apparently they threw wobblers. No, children weren't allowed! Oscar material here—they beat their fists and cried. No, children AREN'T allowed! They got better. They refused to do the exam (which I'd spent days compiling!) unless they saw me. It worked— almost. They got to see me when I was conscious. My mum says that they sat and cried for most of the time that they were there, making everybody really happy. My mum has had to pad and help my memory out here, prompting and reminding. I vaguely remember the huge flower display they gave me, it had balloons in it and a teddy bear. It's a shame that no photographs were taken, I could have shown you how big and clever it was.

I recently read something (that apparently wasn't ghost written) that led one to believe that, when surfacing from a coma you are a bit confused, dazed, as you look around and enquire as to where you are. (TV programmes would spin this out with a tearjerker, broken 'WHY meee . . . blub . . . blub' (that's crying)). I don't THINK so. In three years of rehabilitation, meeting, and living with, the results of various brain traumas (sadly too numerous), I have yet to meet ANYBODY that remembers ANYTHING about 'awakening'—or indeed 'going to sleep' for that matter.

Now let's see if you can follow this. It's my, oh so clever, with it, analogy of a brain trauma. Ready? You are a computer, your brain is the keyboard through which you get the messages to walk, talk, breath, swallow, pee etc etc. The messages relayed by your keyboard (brain) are the actions carried out by your body (computer). Still with me? Now if you got a sledge hammer and smacked the keyboard pretty damned hard, comatose hard, some of your 'keys' might be totally squashed forever, some keys badly bruised and bent out of shape. The 'messages', may be grossly confused and scrambled, tediously deliberate, clumsy and slow or . . . non-existent. Your memory has been, basically, wiped clean. Like being a new-born with a 'clean slate'. Your brain has to relearn everything that you previously didn't think about/took for granted. Walking, talking, breathing . . . pretty basic huh? It depends where you were hit on your keyboard, how hard and which keys were affected, as to whether or not you will be able to spell NORMEL again. Bit clever that huh?

Do you understand what I mean . . . it makes sense to me as I'm the one that's affected by it everyday. Try again, you'll get it right eventually. When you are learning to drive, you firstly have a complete nightmare, moving and avoiding everything else on the road, look in your mirror, break, dip clutch, indicate, change gear, look in mirror, steer, then one day it just comes naturally. In the right order. No problem, if the car isn't damaged.

Often, depending upon the severity and site of the damage, your brain may never remember how to walk again, well not as you did before anyway. One half of your brain, bend your knees, big toes down, lean back slightly—NOT TOO MUCH! hips forward—NOT HEAD! keep your arm down! pick your feet up . . . stupid! There's nothing wrong with your legs, you did it before! Other half, . . . TUT! . . . LOOK! We're GETTING there aren't we?

Yes, I can and do get out and about. Kinda . . . Not quite marathon standard yet, but one day. God, what am I gibbering on about? I wasn't 'marathon' standard before, I was a bit of a, 'take your good health for granted, lazy slob'. Aren't we all to some degree?

I'm a bit of an expert at this head injury stuff now. True, I am not 'au fais' with the technical jargon but I have first hand experience! Beat that! I'm sure that if I had to, I could bullshit quite convincingly. Some people I've met are paid to do that. I recently took my CAT scans (brain X-rays) to a doctor, a 'head' doctor. I asked some questions, like, "What am I looking at and what does it mean?" basically. He held one up to the window, "Well, if it was damaged, what we would be looking for is . . ." Interruption by me, "No . . . it is damaged." He carried on, "Well anyway, if it was damaged . . ." Butted in again, "NO . . . it IS damaged!" At this point, I said something along the, "You haven 't got a clue what you're talking about really, have you?" lines. He admitted that what he did know was too vague for the questions that I had. He specialised in a different area involved in brain injury.

Ooops—I had gone to see him—because I was told to—for something entirely different! I have got an appointment, in a few weeks, with somebody who is trained and specialises in . . . erm . . . brains! He SHOULD be able to answer my questions, but we shall see. I only really have one question I suppose, will I ever be 'normal' again? I think I already know the answer to that one, "No." Well you can't be asleep for a day, week, month, year and really expect to be exactly the same as you were. When you surface, if. But having it in 'black and white' from somebody who knows the textbook stuff, whether verbal or written, is a different matter. Then it's a simple task of admitting it, coping with it and being happy. Any 'self denial' remarks really wind me up! Don't care how they're meant! they're interpreted as taunts, ". . . inappropriate . . ." freaks me too—horrid word.

Those 'in the know' about head injuries are paid to effectively judge me. If anything that I do, or say, is different from how these people would have dealt with situations, the response taken is, "Inappropriate." If you and I were injured in exactly the same spot, in a coma for exactly the same amount of time, to the last minute, we would be totally, completely and utterly, different. Our injury would manifest itself in very different ways, be it physical, mental or both.

(Spruce Girl (another support worker who you will meet later on), has told of a day when we were standing waiting at a pedestrian crossing and she'd told me, "To watch out for the lorry!" "Why?" I'd answered).

Memory seems to be a common denominator—for head injuries (just reminding you, that's what I'm waffling on about). We weren't the same beforehand—surely—so why on earth should we, apart from the head injury, be alike in any other way now? Yes OK, there are vague similarities, walking, talking, memory, speech, co-ordination, . . . gosh there are loads! BUT, they are vague, and at the end of that day, as I said earlier, you and I would be different.

People around were worried I was depressed. Everybody gets too fed up sometimes. When something as devastating as this happens to you and you are becoming aware of how it affects you daily, you have more right than most to be a bit miserable sometimes. They had witnessed a day when I seemed to be sobbing every other sentence. Obviously heartbroken at the time. If I was 'bouncing' about being irritatingly happy all the time . . . then worry, I concluded. That particular specialist must have been quite happy with that, haven't seen him since. Not that I'm racked off with the innuendos that I really have perfected the art of sitting on my backside, and talking out of it, at the same time! Not that I've been extraordinarily frustrated by lots (millions!) of things and people over the last three years. Mostly me. Playing squash with Pathetic nearly always ended with him saying, "Sod this" and just stomping off the court. Where I would stubbornly 'play' on my own, having a great time for a few minutes, until I was bored with losing. Bit melodramatic—I can no longer do this, woe is me (back of hand on forehead for full effect). One day you'll realise that maybe, you just don't have the choice anymore.

I'm actually quite happy to sit on my—ever spreading—backside, drinking coffee and smoking fags all day. Acting out 'novelist'. Nobody will have to buy this 'book' because its been read to and by EVERYBODY, ALL the time! My mum's eyes now glaze over if you say 'book'. "I've read it, a MILLION times!" "But I've changed it!" is always my cunning reply. Mum's good at this now too, "Not THAT much!" I'm quite enjoying this. You should all try it. Writing a 'book'—NOT having a head injury. Though there are a few who should really try that out as well. See what it's like for real, EVERY day.

Now, will this ever be a finished and published piece? Will it ever get out of my den? Who knows? Who knows . . . I say this ALL the time. Why, "Who knows?" Do you do that? Have certain phrases, sayings that you use/say all the time? Each time that you 'fall prey' again . . . noooo! Whenever people find out that I'm a trained teacher, and they cope with that, they ALWAYS ask, "What did you teach?" I ALWAYS answer, "Children." Always, I can't think of any other answer though! Not that I've tried. So, back to the point!—the book!

I woke up, from the best excuse I've ever had for time off work and a long lie in! Bit extreme, granted. Maybe I should ring in with a 'headache' next time? Anyway, I woke up. My memories are very selective, very vague and some have been 'filled in' by family and friends etc.

Gillian spent the first six weeks after her accident in a coma. She was semi-conscious for a further month. In September 1994, she returned to the UK and lived with her parents before spending a number of months in hospital on a weekly basis.

So, I was in a Mid-Eastern country, Pathetic (aka my then-husband), was working in another nearby country. We had the perfect marriage, lived in different countries. Still do! Only we spoke sometimes then. (Pathetic—I'll explain this later, don't doubt me). I was teaching, children (ha!), driving home from a night out with friends. (Still don't really know where I'd been or with whom). I have been told, numbers of times, still don't really know where I'd been, or with whom. Aided, prompted and otherwise, these are my memories. They have little or no order at all, in my mind, although they'll get sorted on paper (I hope).

Mum says that I had a catheter and that the tube kept getting blocked with 'fatty stuff'. Thickish, whitish and disturbing. I was indicating discomfort although I didn't/couldn't say anything. My mum did. The nurses looked, 'it was OK—normal'. Mum says that I kept grumbling and that the tube kept getting blocked. She says that she would sit and squash this 'fat' through the tube. She wasn't happy—she told them, in no uncertain terms. A specialist Doctor came round, "Take it out, now!" was ordered. I was due for damaged kidneys. Lovely. Mum got the 'I told you so!' T-shirt out again.

I'm told that I also had a feeding tube that I wasn't too happy with. Having had my wrists slapped for touching it, my family were horrified when I'd got a smug, rrsssp, (phonetic raspberry!) smirk on my face and was holding, and dangling, the offending tube in my hand. Nice one! The nurses put it back. Mum says they eventually got bored, it wasn't staying in. Where would we be without mums? Well, we wouldn't really, would we? But I've got my mum to thank more than once.

Mum says I always had my head turned to the right. Any attempts made by ANYBODY to forcibly correct this resulted in whimpers, snarls and general unpleasantness. I would defiantly swing my sight to the right. So upon my mum's insistence I had my neck X-rayed as she feared it may be damaged. My bed, with me, had to be pushed to the appropriate department where my mum was told, had my neck been shorter it would have been broken in the collision. I have no memory of this incident.

Present in body, not in mind. Mum had to apparently sit on me on the bed to hold me still. No apparent snags, but my neck still troubles me, but not so much that I miss everything on my left. I can keep my eyes forward now. I did get serious double vision—weird! It's OK now, most of the time. (I did go and see an optician regarding this and found out that my right eye is damaged. It looks OK to me). Double vision troubles me, and everyone else! when I'm drunk or really tired. I was in total disbelief when I was told this! No! Apparently, I would spasm, or just throw my legs around—as you do, if you can— without underwear on! Evidently I was almost doing the can-can, with a lascivious leer, whenever a certain male visitor came. No! My brother and mum would have been there to witness this bed show too! Tart! I don't recall liking him, the target, THAT much! It wasn't Pathetic (who went back to work, in another country, the moment my mum arrived. Work, obviously, being more important). So, my mum and brother had to cope alone, in a strange country, strange being the operative word!

Their hero was a male friend (Gadget Boy) who I had met recently. He chaperoned them, protected, advised and was there. So they weren't alone. By all accounts, if it wasn't for him they would have had a complete nightmare on top of the situation with me. He reminded me of the first time we met. I was ordering a drink at the bar of a club for expatriates of all nationalities. He grabbed one of my hands and scrutinised it. They were both intricately painted with henna designs. They had been done, I elaborated, at my school summer fete that day. "It's always summer!" he joked, then started chatting, telling me that my hands would be like this for days. I saw him again, we chatted. He wrote a poem for me, which he didn't give to me until after my accident:

> A beautiful smile, a casual glance
> A polite word or two, how she enchants
> We talk and we laugh, sorry what was your name
> The girl and I are playing the game
> We laugh and smile and begin to sing

The day the beautiful girl walked in
A chance meeting again, she remembers my name
I remember her all as we play on the same
We stay late that night and talk, a delight
The beautiful girl has not taken flight
Such clumsy words though the meanings so true
We're all alone now and not sure what to do
Moving too fast with our thoughts racing past
Now's the time to part, so empty my heart
We share some more time as we wine and dine
Sharing talk of before she enchants once more
and we laugh and we smile telling jokes for a while
Then we move from the throng, the people are gone
We kiss as we part, how she tears at my heart

"What's the title?"—if it had one? I asked him. "Erm . . . Beautiful girl . . . or something . . ." he smiled.
Ahh—I like him.
He likes four wheel driving in sand-dunes and has a posh path-finding gadget, it can get you anywhere from anywhere, apparently, providing of course you know where you are (I 'm still lost when I get to the end of my road, especially market day when one stumbles about aimlessly for a few hours with a pocket full of lists). He is a useful oddity collector therefore, from hereon, he will be referred to as, drumroll, Gadget Boy (so now you know).

Well, I was moved, apparently, shortly after I surfaced and before we got to grand scale performance bed shows, from intensive care to a normal ward. I got a lot of attention, I was the only white, non Muslim female in my ward. Tall too—only five feet seven inches—but Titan nevertheless! The physiotherapist that tried desperately to lug me around, that was funny—you had to be there! He was about five feet two inches, just imagine—tall, clumsy, deadweight, female, (me). I called him Doctor Zhivago, of course that wasn't his real name! I couldn't remember his real name—something foreign. Something probably as hard to say as to remember. Bored with keep telling me, or realizing that it was a pretty pointless exercise, he answered to 'Doctor Zhivago'. He seemed quite happy to do so, it was easier and I had told him that he reminded me of the male hero, lead in the film. My mum tells me that he always carried a packet of Chicklets chewing gum in his overall top pocket. I never asked, I'd just help myself with a cheeky lop-sided smirk! Who could reprimand, or be cross? I liked him. Even when I was put on a conveyer-belt walking machine. I lasted, ooh what, two seconds max—from 'ignition' to 'landing', in a rather unladylike heap at my mum's feet—at the end of the treadmill. My mum says, "It wasn't even two seconds!" It was turned on, I came off.

On the ward—the memories that I have retained, make me wish that I had been more 'with it'. To have noticed, and remembered more. I had to go to the toilet, well I hadn't 'been' for six weeks. I HAD to go. Which meant that I had to crash into the wheelchair and be taken. Thankfully, my mum was there and had the joy of sitting through this experience with me. Well, having to hold me onto the toilet she had no choice really. She says, "It was six weeks worth!—a privilege to have witnessed and shared!" There I was, having my own nightmare, one half of my brain saying, "Gillian you NEED to go to the toilet, NOW really." the other half, "Yeah . . . but, what do we do again?" So, who cares if we stay on the toilet or not?

So, we got there. Two nurses followed us in. I said, "Could you please leave, and close the door." or thought I did. They stayed. Maybe they didn't hear me, "PLEASE GO, AND CLOSE THE DOOR." They stayed. No, it's happening! "FUCK OFF." They left, and my mum had a verbal fit. BUT, it worked. I can go to the toilet all on my own now! I've been potty trained again.

It was a very religious country, so your bed had curtains you could pull around to aid privacy, thus creating your own 'space'. Well, a visitor next door had the back of his chair pushed against my bed, with the curtain caught. Irritated, I (honestly) meant to just nudge him to move his chair forward. What actually happened was that I jerked, and fell, whilst trying to lean forward, and ended up punching him. Oops! Turning to look at my family, with a shrug on my shoulders, they looked gobsmacked. I, tongue tied my explanation—that, "He was in my space . . . he was in my space!" My brother's reply, "Yeah . . . so why did you punch him?"

Oh oh . . . Pathetic, brought in some cigarettes, rolling tobacco and papers for me. He visited every other weekend, when he could spare the time from work. How thoughtful, ahh. My mum went berserk, she, 'didn't know she smoked'! Well, she does now! To have a fix meant tackling the wheelchair, getting somebody to take me off the ward, sit with me and bring me back. A real bind. The cigarettes ran out, onto the roll ups. Fix time . . . "Could somebody roll me a cig please?" Silence. "No . . ." "Please." I whimpered. "No, do it yourself." was the reply. So I did. Those around my bed looked on, whilst I 'rolled' what looked like a Havana and a tampon crossed. They made me smoke it too. I think that my yellow fingers are from that day.

Incidentally, as a smoker is there anything worse than having twenty fags and NO LIGHT! Go on, hands up how many of you have melted facial hair on the toaster/cooker? Vice versa you can always find a nice juicy tab in the ashtray, or bin, or . . .

An obviously distressed, and pained, patient was moaning loudly and in turn distressing the rest of the ward. Well, pigging me off at least. My mum went over to comfort her. She quietened the girl down. "What's wrong with her?" I asked when she came back. "WHAT? She's making all that noise and she's only had her APPENDIX out?" I had MY appendix out when I was NINE. Nothing to it!—WHINGEY BAG! I'm still a very tolerant, sympathetic, suffer fools gladly type of person.

I had a Walkman, a gift. Pathetic bought it for me so that MY tapes could be played to me subconsciously. I never saw it—it was stolen. My wedding and engagement rings were stolen too. They weren't big or clever but, they were mine. That's pretty low, I was in a coma for goodness sake. Here's me thinking that if you're in a coma, elderly, disabled—disadvantaged in any way—that you were exempt from this kind of spiteful, thoughtless, pettiness. Wrong! Silly cow! Wrong!

Some of the nurses really were in the right job. My mum tells me that when I was asleep (I had long, straight hair) the nurses would tie my hair up differently each day using bandages. My mum says that my hair was bright red. I'd recently hennaed it with a 'natural' colourant that was 'temporary' and 'washed out gradually'—in about a year! The nurses had great fun playing 'hairdressers' every day. I'm glad they were having fun, making me look like a turnip one day, a palm tree the next. No, I am glad. I went into the intensive care unit a year later, saw nurses who were my best friends, they had big, big grins: "Jeeel, how are yoo?" My mum knew who they were, and was beside herself all the time we were there. She kept making sweeping gestures in my direction, with a YES!! grin. Me? Oh I was hanging onto something in the background, with a lop-sided, vacant grin on my face.

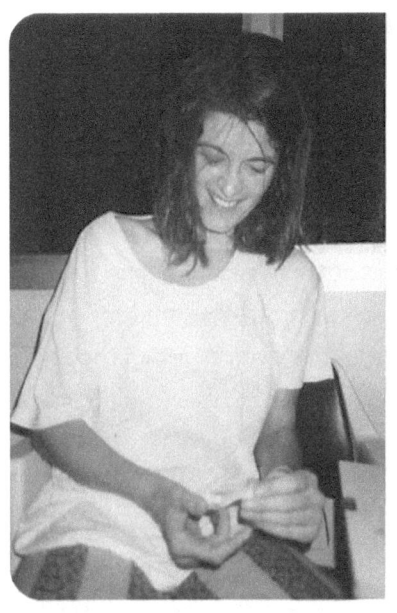

Desperate measures,
how much tobacco?

20 minutes later . . .

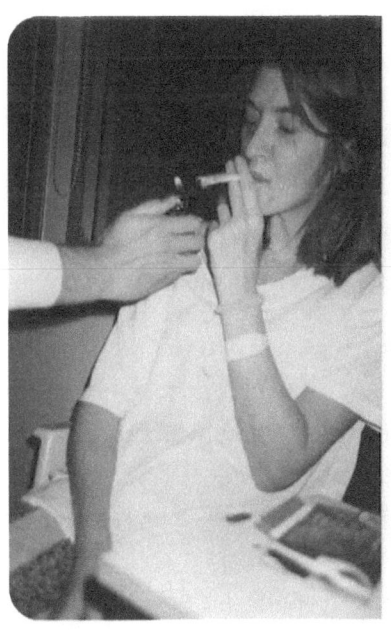

da da . . . we have a 'fag'

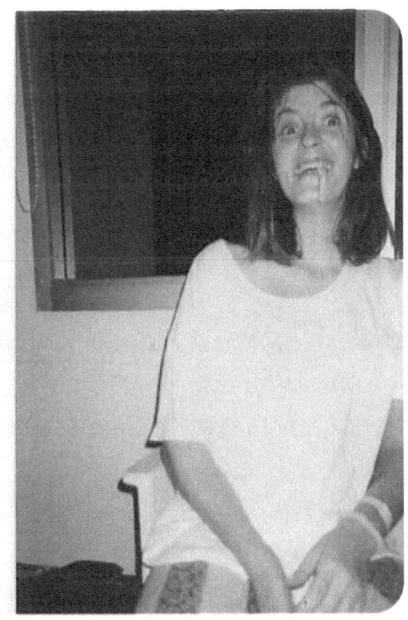

the big smoke!!!

Intensive care. It's unpleasantly unnerving, there is nothing! No noise, no movement. There were no other visitors whilst I was there. I'm quite glad really, only mechanical noises, otherwise TOTAL, still, silence. Unnerving. Have any of you seen the film 'Patrick'? An eerie film in which a comatose young man is controlling his surroundings and people, using electricity producing brain waves.

I wasn't really 'with it' until we got to the normal ward—where I'd had my eyes open. They all grinned, they all asked how I was, and my mum, all of them had a 'wow' look on their faces, in their voices, when they first saw and recognised me.

I had been conscious for a month now and was getting to know the faces of the nurses on my ward. I remember the name of one, Esmet, I remember her as cheery soul that made me laugh. She gave me a tape of music when I left to go home, a tape of popular love songs. I think she was one of the nurses that followed mum and I into the bathroom that time and I told her to, "Fuck off!" She understood.

I was still all over the place on two sticks, but without them I just could not stand up without someone or something to hold onto, to drag myself up, then to stay up. All in all, I am seriously happy that I went and did that visit—it was a total ego trip. What a buzz! Although Dr Zchivago wasn't there, I had hoped he would be, needing him to say 'Wow'. Esmet wasn't there either.

Oh yeah, a serious head injury and you turn into Pavlov's dog! On the ward, breakfast was always at eight. Although I don't dribble uncontrollably at the sound of bells, I still wake up at eight. One half of my brain, 'go back to sleep, we don't have to get up . . .' Other half, drooling, 'YES! we do. It's eight in the morning that's why!' I get up and have a coffee and cigarette.

A friend bought me some juggling balls, I could juggle with three before the accident—NOT any more. They were for me to squeeze in my hands, if I could KEEP HOLD OF THEM! If I could have thrown them, imagine—the windows, the nurses, fellow (ill) patients, visitors . . . that would have been good eh? "Oops! oops! . . . sorry . . . oops." But, I couldn't. Still can't. It was discovered, quite by accident, that I could roll one of the balls up my leg, using the other leg/foot. I wanted the ball and nobody was listening to me. Apparently I liked the very jubilant reaction so much, that I did it for everybody and anybody—all the time. Probably with no underwear on! Who needs to juggle?

I've said it was a religious country. As a result I often had strangers, friends, visitors (sometimes mine) and work colleagues wailing round my bed for me. I was touched (for about five minutes), then I wanted to go for a cigarette. My mum was having a nervous breakdown. My brother, having deserved and needing time out from medical hospital stuff, went out with his new (also inebriated!), mates, for an adventure—on a fast, speed boat. He apparently fell so badly he was lucky to only have a scarily amazing bruise on his arm/shoulder/elbow/hand. Apparently he was just lucky. So my mum, at this point had a complete fit, with everything and everybody, apparently. She deserved to, nobody had the right to judge. Nobody did.

One visit, there was just my brother. I needed a wee, I had wheedled, begged, offered money for him to agree to take me for a cigarette, after the bathroom. All the right stuff? Fag, lighter. I pulled myself off the bed and upright (no I didn't—I was man-handled by my brother). He joked, I started laughing, "No . . . I'm gonna wet myself!" I giggled. My brother panicked, "Oh no . . . hold it in!" "I can't!" was the reply. At this point I was pushed (or did she fall?) backwards onto my bed—which I had just got off—that had an incontinence sheet for just such mishaps. He says that I was sprawled, ungainly on the bed, literally wetting myself with laughter. He was having a complete breakdown, "I could see a yellow fountain!" and mum was due! "Bloody hell . . . no." I don't think my mum knows to this day (she does now). So, thank someone for incontinence sheets, elasticated waists and microwaves!

I was in this (the first) hospital for two and a half months. I cannot recall having a wash, or brushing my teeth ONCE. Come to think of it, I only remember going to the toilet that one time!

My mum tells me that when I was first being fed, to try and get my taste buds going, they went out and got some strained baby food. Yummy! By all accounts it hit the bed, the floor, me, my mum, the nurses—I didn't like it. I liked the mass produced, cheap hospital mince that was always cold when it got to me. Perfect. I was eating by myself again. Which was a pretty hit or miss affair—my mouth and anybody near.

**** drinking and eating again on my own—almost ****

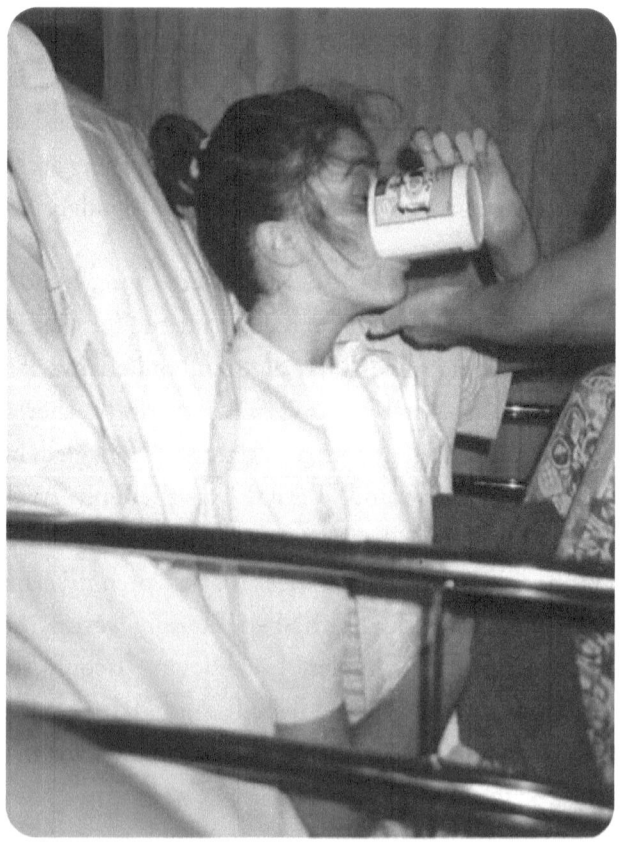

Time to fly back to the UK.

CHAPTER TWO

A visit to my flat before we go, to see if I remembered anything. I knew where I was, because I was told, and recognised a few things. Packed some clothing, none of which fits me any more. Gillian Mark One was a skinny bitch!

Before the accident I was living in a different foreign country to my husband. I had no job but I did have two cats. Schwarma (Arabic for kebab—as in, she'd be one if she made a horrid mess anywhere. Pathetic said this, not me). She had to be an indoor cat, boy was she spoilt. We bought her a cat lead, we tried it out in the flat. We put the lead on her. She was standing behind Pathetic, he started walking. She promptly threw herself on her back attacking the lead. He didn't notice, he dragged her down the corridor and kept yanking the lead, ". . . because she's pulling!" No, she's not doing anything, YOU'RE pulling HER. We never took her out. Not beaten, I got her a playmate, a new kitten. Cute . . . Pathetic's reaction was: "Gillian are you mad? bloody hell. Rat one (pointing at Schwarma), and Rat two!! Need I say more?" So I named the new kitten Ratatouille. Good huh?

The other half only tolerated them for me. YES! I cleaned out their litter tray, fed them, 'treated' them. If he called Number One, God, she would come from NOWHERE, sit on his chest, purr as though he was made of catnip, and desperately try and shove her nose up his! Tart, she never did that to me. I saw them a year later, quite happy thank you, who are you again? I was actually a bit hurt that they didn't seem to know who I was. Or they did, yeah she's the one that left us for days, no food, no water, full litter tray . . . bag! I really don't know what happened to them. I do know that the couple who took them in split up, no real surprise there, but my cats? I don't think about it.

Gillian, skinny show off, on honeymoon (1992)

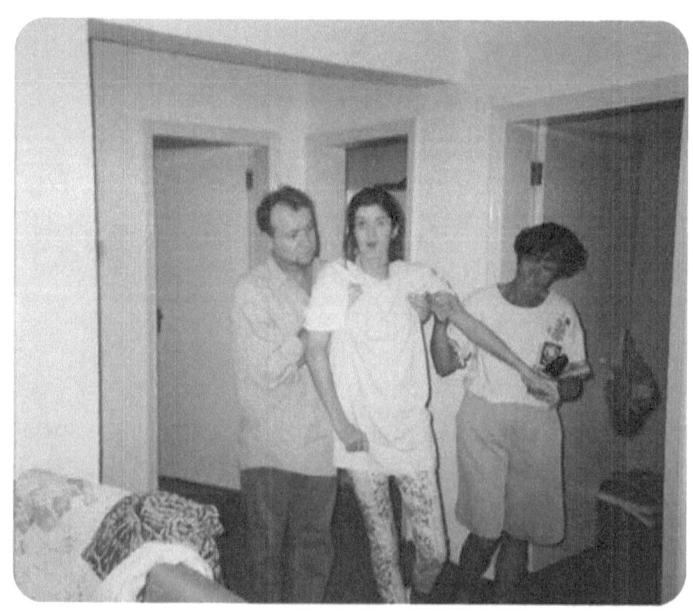

Coming out of the bathroom and getting ready to go home (1994)

So, my flat was mobile with cat fleas. I think my brother still has some bite marks. The front room—in fact, the whole flat—was poky, dark (no windows), in a horrid neighbourhood and looked worse than a student bed sit. It was a sad dump basically. My mum had a great time, cleaning, polishing, anything really to try and distract her thoughts from her baby hanging onto life with mechanical aids. She had nearly three months of this, good job my flat was such a nightmare. I remembered why I'd got this horrid flat. Pathetic was living in a rent paid mansion—well in comparison to this hovel anyway—I wasn't working, and it was all I could afford at the time. I just never got around to moving when I was working, that's all! I was therefore really pleased that I was reminded of my 'home'. A memory I shall bloody keep forever. I've got a memory snag yes . . . BUT can I forget my luxurious, flea infested digs?

Seriously, we've got a flight to catch to soggy England, didn't we ought to get out of here? An hour early? We can have coffee or something!

Well, the airport—remember that we were in a hot (very hot) country, my mum, brother, hand luggage and a sack of spuds who really didn't care as long as she could have another 'fix'. The airport staff suggested that instead of walking they could give us a lift on the luggage trailer—with the luggage . . . Yes please! Our transport to the plane: wheelchair, me, mum, brother, hand luggage—all on the back of a luggage carrier, with the luggage! My mum and brother had to hold the chair on, or rather hold me into the chair. The chair was perfectly still. I was taken by wheelchair to the aeroplane door, then transferred into a special wheelchair that fits between the aisles, to get to my seat. I was the first on and off. It was quite a long flight and, man get this, I didn't need to get up for a wee once! I was asleep most of the flight. Awake getting on, eating, and getting off. Nicely, a simple life this is what we like! We had to change flights, therefore change of wheelchair, customs, language etc. Oh goody, my life's too simple, I should bugger it up a bit more. Nah, let somebody else do it. Airport officials had to keep tabs on the wheelchair, in case we ran away with it. So my mum and I ended up upstairs with the chair, keeping it company, and my brother was downstairs—somewhere—with our passports and money. My mum was having a breakdown again. I was asking everybody if they had a light? I was having my own crisis.

I don't really remember the flight, or my dad picking us up from the airport.

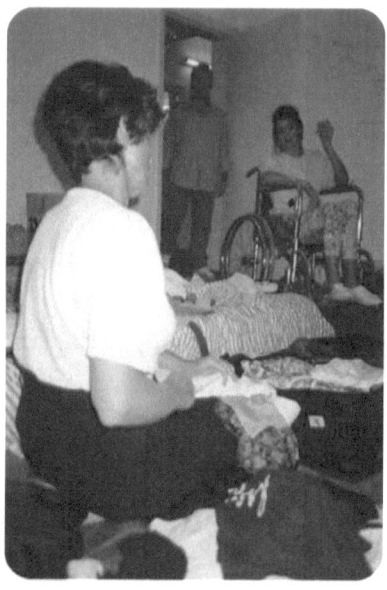

having a cig' playing dictator

At the airport, sack of puds and entourage . . .

I love the take-off, the landing, the in-flight meals (all those little packets), flying basically. One day I was going to get an aviator's licence. The only thing that stopped me before was . . . money. Is it a sad sign of the times that every scenario in our lives, good or bad, boils down to the same thing . . . money (I did fall for the salesman spiel once. I had a bash at selling insurance. Yes! I could make millions—I was crap at it. Looked the part, but was crap. I don't think I bothered much—I did enough to get by, keep my nose clean as it were. Should have sold myself some).

If I wasn't eating, where did the two stones I gained come from? Because you were pretty immobile in a wheelchair? Not because you ate a bar of chocolate every day?—well I could swallow it! and it tasted nice. Two stones! I suddenly discovered what bras were for and that I'd been wearing it back to front all these years! I know why men are so fascinated now, I was transfixed! The novelty soon wore off, they get in the way and you get the big fat stomach and bum to go with them. I didn't notice, or care really until going through my wardrobe. I realized that nothing I had fitted me anymore—not even vaguely. Each item when tried on (if it got past my bum), the button and fastener were miles apart! The replacement wardrobe was an unflattering array of elastic waist tents. Time to cut down on the chocolate I feel, be hard fatty, just one bar a day! I maybe ought to cut down on the fags too, one packet per day! It's sad how many smokers, with a head injury, keep our government afloat by the amount of tax they pay as chain-smokers! I identify with this, one smokes as one CAN, you can't really freak, and smack somebody, if you've got a 'fire' in your hand. If I'd even tried to smack anybody, I would have fallen over. Oh yeah, I'm a nicotine addict too.

So, back home. My brother had to stay with me, as I just couldn't do normal things alone or safely. Drink coffee and smoke, this could be done unaided, a skill almost perfected. My parents had to bug somebody about the wheelchair, then they had to go and pick it up. Grab-rails were fitted up the stairs, so I could grab and pull myself up unaided. Grab-rail over the toilet, so something wasn't broken each time I had a wee, thus reducing the amount of accidents and the subsequent laundry. Getting in and out of the bath, even with the hydraulic bath chair, was a real ordeal that couldn't be done alone (at this time my hair had to be washed for me too). The back door (front door wasn't used), had steps leading to the outside. So that I wasn't confined, grab-rails were fitted, even though I couldn't walk—they were much used later.

My mum, eventually had to go back to work. Well, the threat of no job to go back to if it wasn't soon, NOW, sorted that one. Dad was working. Fortunately my brother, basically, had nothing better to do than make and carry coffee and man-handle a useless, fat, moaning lump around and up Mount Everest. I should have installed a chair, kettle and ashtray in the bathroom. Almost each time I empty my bladder, I fill it up again. Well, if I'm up anyway might as well put the kettle on! Sorted!

I couldn't even go to the toilet on my own, nightmare! Each time I went, my brother had to almost carry me up the mountain. No mean feat! I was fast becoming a weeble shape—but I wobbled and fell down. Lots of people came to look at me, one of them being a physiotherapist who suggested and showed me how to get up and down the stairs on my bum. Took ages, I had to set off ten minutes before I actually wanted the bathroom. But, I got there. As a result of these observations I ended up in another hospital, for an intensive rehabilitation agenda.

I stayed in the hospital during the week and went home for the weekends—when my family had the time to cope and look after me. I wasn't 'ill', so I didn't need to stay there when the physios and OTs (Physiotherapists and Occupational Therapists) were off for the weekend. I wasn't sick/ill, I was brain damaged. So, again, I was in 'residence' with sick people. One of those weekends home, my brother and I sat on the back doorstep one night, having a smoke, chatting and putting the world to rights. It was a clean, clear night. I said, rather poignantly, "If anything ever happens to either one of us, remember this night." He forgot.

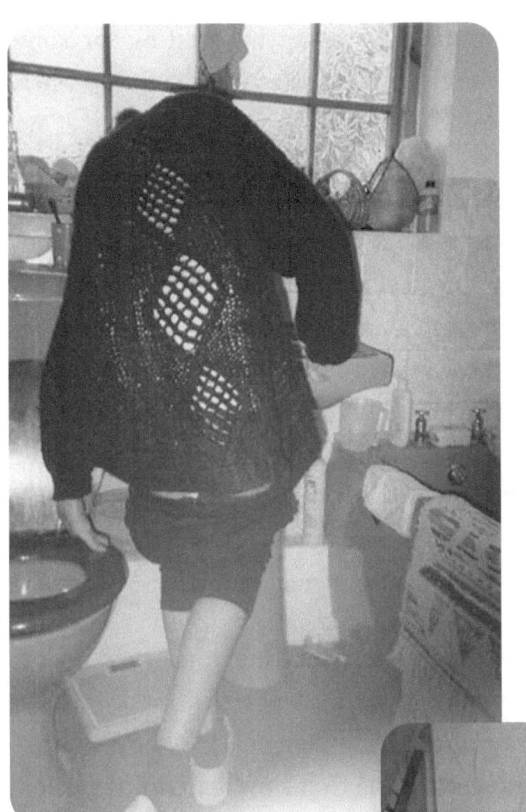

My brother took this . . .
thank you! . . .
of me takling the toilet.

Tackling mount Everest

In physio, one day, an elderly patient was sitting waiting for some attention and to have a session on the parallel bars. She fell asleep where she was sitting with her arms folded—brilliant.

It was fast becoming known that if there was coffee anywhere, I generally wouldn't be far away. Ready, cig and light, Gillian Mark two was a boy scout! They had biscuits too! Wey hey! I could taste sweet. "Gillian, if you try really hard, you'll get over the damage and be skiing again—one day." I'm sorry, but no matter how many times you say this to yourself, or hear it, crashing about, falling and hurting is BORING. Then one gets accused of 'self denial', by women who dye their hair red! I was asked recently if my hair was coloured? If they do brown with silver flashes, yes. This person also said my hair, "Looks nice down." It's nearly always up and out of the way, must have been having a good hair day.

Swimming—I KNOW that it's 'good' for you. But from scuba diving, being in a synchronised swimming team, diving in backwards—swimming in pain, and like a brick, is saddening. Didn't know what to feel when swimming was arranged for the first time, a disabled session. It all started to feel 'iffy' when support had to be given to undress me. Got to the edge of the pool. Hey, I remember how this felt! With gold fish eyes, one of the pool attendants was becoming my Siamese twin. I didn't know what to do! In my mind, scuba diving and graceful; in reality, my arms and legs weren't talking to each other and I had to keep being reminded that I could touch the bottom! Being dressed, I was chuntering and grumbling (no disrespect) that ninety percent of this swimming group were mentally disabled and could swim! Left upset, disappointed and feeling the odd one out. Where do you fit? Where can you go? What CAN you do? It upset me enough to make excuses not to go again for a while. I will go again, one day . . . maybe. If I want to.

As part of the Occupational Therapy (OT), I had to plan, buy the ingredients for, follow a recipe, prepare a meal, and then eat it! I chose to make spaghetti bolognese. Nobody in my family was at all surprised. In fact they told me what I'd cooked when I said I had been cooking. Well, it took me ages, it was very messy and clumsy, but I got there. It was very nice. Of course it was! It is, to this day, still the only meal I can cook on auto pilot. As a student I would make a large batch and be quite happy to eat it for days. When I went to see Pathetic alone, nineteen months after my injury and excitedly told him, "That I could cook spaghetti bolognese!" I then asked him, 'did he want some?' (I really meant that he was getting some, whether he wanted it or not). "No." he flatly declined. I asked why? He didn't like it. I thought that he did. He explained that when you have it almost every day for the first three months of your marriage, you tend to go off it. Oh. He was exaggerating for effect, I think (Wimp). I have, on and off, been making it for ten years, and I still like it! So if you're ever invited for dinner and you don't like 'spag bog'—bring sandwiches.

In one of the OT sessions I was painting—with RED paint. It couldn't really be any other colour in a hospital could it? One of the porters was wandering about, talking to the patients. He was wearing a green tie, with artistic splodges of red paint. There I was caught red handed, literally, and red faced and red haired and red clothed . . . Anyway, I thought it made his tie look better. Bloody amazing! and I have NO idea how that happened. Every 'art' session after that, though, a 'Danger Gillian painting!' notice was stuck on the door. Forewarned is forearmed? I think I still managed to get a patient or two. I, in turn, was wheeled out of these 'playtimes' looking like a rainbow sprite. Other playtimes—Darts. We weren't allowed pointy ones that stayed in the board! They were velcro and about half of mine actually hit the board and two of those scored. A waste of time.

A night out to the theatre was organised as one of the OTs was appearing in the show, '42nd Street', an all singing, all dancing production. It was weird seeing her on stage as it was totally out of context. She had a life outside the OT uniform, which bothered me—I don't really know how, or why. They had a raffle in the interval and the lady that won approached me holding out the prize, which was a set of Waterford crystal. She gave the glasses to me as I was "So brave!" I didn't know what for, but what a nice thing to do!

In the physio I was still wobbling about alarmingly. They tried me with a walking frame. I kept being found on my back, on the floor, still clutching the frame. Usually sniggering confusedly. Often surrounded by something that was once whole. Never seemed to hurt myself really badly, as in broken bones badly, was thankfully only jarred, bruised and scratched—oops! They took the frame off me. I was really crap in doorways anyway! Back to the chair.

I was wearing Pathetic's jeans. I could fasten them and they went with my flat, brown, suede boots. Which are in the cobblers every other week being re-heeled! Well I can walk in them! Anything else feels like STILTS! One day in physio I was doing a Michelin Man impression, with my T-shirt raised. I wailed, "LOOK at this (prod, prod, wobble wobble) forty two inch waist, and they're TIGHT on me! No!" I repeated this to Pathetic on the phone, "Cheeky cow—they're THIRTY two!" he exclaimed. Oh . . . still THIRTY TWO inches! Size ten to a hundred in ONE year! This is what we like, nice round figures, nice round body. Mellow, round, comfy, curved. No, fat cow!

Around this time I had my first period since the accident. My ovaries woke up—so, what do we do with all this gunge again? Throw it away! OK . . . now what do we do? We use mattresses that's what we do! I was in physio one day, lying on my back, raising my legs in the air. Why not? if you can. I kept getting quite a sharp pain. The 'mattress' had roamed around and stuck itself to me—so each time I raised my leg I was effectively plucking myself. I was nearly bald. With absolute horror, I can recall the first time I used a tampon again. My mum had to do it for me to remind me what to do. Just had to. No more bedding for me!

I discovered that I could get off the toilet without grabbing the rail or radiator to drag myself up, and then stay up. Shouting, "MUM!" she came so quick that she must have been stood outside the door! "Are you alright? What's wrong?" she demanded. I was sitting, grinning, on the toilet. "Watch this!" I then stood up and crashed back down, giggled then stood up and crashed back down, then stood up and my mum said, "Alright, I've seen it now! stop it or you'll break the toilet!"

My mum and brother visited me in the hospital midweek. Once my dad came along and it was horrendous! Talk about atmosphere. My parents were at serious loggerheads. It WASN'T my accident—though I'm sure it didn't help. They 'celebrated' their thirtieth Wedding Anniversary and that was that—they'd done their time—they're divorced now.

Opposite my bay in the ward was the smoker's room! Seriously handy, spent most of my spare time in there. It was such an effort to get in there in the first place, it was easier to just stay there. Once in the wheelchair, the wheels couldn't be reached so had to 'paddle' my feet to get anywhere. The physios went nuts about this habit, I was covered in bruises because I have a nicotine habit. Well, they were all sick and in pain in the ward— except for me. Eyesight (double vision) and memory meant I couldn't read. Believe me it's head-numbing having to re-read pages, usually the first chapter, to remind yourself what's going on with who. Reading the first chapter for a week, every day ... try it, with your favourite book. I got six books out of the library, in year four of this account, to try again. Things I knew I had read before and knew I had liked. I rang twice to get them re-dated. They all went back late, unread.

One weekend home I was at the local pub. Wobbling en route to the toilet. A young boy saw me, he pushed his mum out of my way, "Watch out! her legs don't work!" What's that saying—'the innocence of babes'? Literal naivety. A skill we sadly lose with age and circumstance. In the same pub, there were two young girls in the toilets, sneaking a fag. Furtive glances and stifled giggles, they waited until I was in the cubicle. "Did you see the state?" I did think of going out and saying, 'I wish ... etc etc ...' I could have had a field day, as it were. When I came out, they had gone, wouldn't have said anything anyway—not that bothered and wanted to get back! Oh, and they looked stupid. Funny, as I'd had a drink, or two.

My family all tried spaghetti bolognese with me, literally. Well, each family meal there was a fat, mummy sitting at the table. I was 'armed' with a gaudy plastic apron, a bath towel over my knees (essential! They all had to be dyed after the bolognese adventure), and a woolly hat, to stop me eating my hair and getting food in it. Armed to tackle the nearly cold pre-cut cardboard—trying to cut food myself meant slipping with the knife and emptying my plate onto the table or my knees. My sense of taste and smell were affected meaning that only sweet, savoury and cheese could be distinguished. Too weird, but that was it. I had difficulty swallowing too, so no crispy, crunchy tasty, flaky food for me! (I can feel and know when I am going to choke, cough and splutter—I mean splatter! anyone near with the chewed up contents of my mouth!—but cannot react quickly enough to stop it and to do anything about it). OH NO! Semi-cold, tasteless slop for me please. The sad thing is that everything tasted the same to me for a long time. These senses are normal now—well normal to me anyway. I fortunately like cheese. It's interesting a lot of people that I know with a head injury, have a real taste for incredibly hot curries—the hotter the better.

Christmas came and the token tinsel started to appear around the hospital as did the fluffy animal Xmas cards. Suitably fired and motivated I had this brilliant idea. I know, lets lug me and the chair, at the busiest time of the year, in the cold, round all the packed, gaudy 'cheapo' shops! So I can 'rise' to my challenge. To buy all the physios, OTs, doctors, nurses on my ward, speech therapists, porters—a Xmas gift each for ninety nine pence! What a brilliant idea! So, my mum honoured my whim and traipsed around lots of shops with me for hours. My challenge was met, nicely, and we fully utilised the chair. All the weight on my knees kept me in too.

This first Christmas was the first time I had used a hairdryer since the accident. Getting ready for an evening out and making myself into a 'glamour puss'. I pointed it towards my head, as you do. I was sitting down, so I didn't have to think about standing as well. There was a horrendous smell of burning hair, my very long fringe was stuck in the back of the hairdryer, Oops. Turned it off and started laughing. When I let go of the hairdryer it was dangling from my head in my hair. My mum had to untangle me and since it was always tied up, out of the way, you couldn't see the fuzzy bit. I still never use the hairdryer, I still just tie my hair up when it's wet from being washed. See, I was setting routines in my life very early on. An incredibly stupid routine if I go to bed like this—I get up the next day looking like velcro.

Pathetic came home for my first Xmas, as I am now. It was OK, I think. Well, nothing striking either way that I remember anyway. We're seven months down the line here—he hadn't seen me for five of those. It was a shitty time, and he missed it. He wasn't there, in body either. Pathetic had been for Xmas and I was still getting intermittent saddening phone calls from him. Which were 'costing a fortune!' well he was paying for the car! and the phone calls were WEEKLY! Sad.

Now, I'm completely lost . . . stay with me. I have to. But where are the rules, guide-lines, instructions on how to deal with, and what to expect when things like this happen? Things—head injuries, childbirth, bereavement, divorce . . . the list IS endless. So what to do? What to say? To whom? Frustrating, is a weak and pathetic word. I'm not the only one—we've all got our 'crosses to bear'.

I'll share this with you . . .

A Crabbit Old Woman Wrote This:

> What do you see nurses, what do you see?
> Are you thinking when you are looking at me—
> a crabbit old woman, not very wise,
> Uncertain of habit with faraway eyes,
> Who dribbles her food and makes no reply,
> When you say in a loud voice—
> "I do wish you'd try!"

Who seems not to notice the things that you do,
And forever is losing a stocking or shoe.
Who unresisting or not, lets you do as you will,
With bathing and feeding the long day to fill.
Is that what you are thinking?
Is that what you see?
Then open eyes, nurse, you're not looking at me.
I'll tell you who I am as I sit here so still.
As I use at your bidding, as I eat at your will.
I'm a small child of ten with a father and mother,
Brothers and sisters that love one another.
A young girl of sixteen with wings on her feet,
Dreaming that soon now a lover she'll meet.
A bride soon at twenty—my heart gives a leap,
Remembering the vows that I promised to keep.
At twenty five now I have young of my own,
Who need me to build a secure happy home—
A woman of thirty, my young now grow fast,
Bound to each other with ties that should last.
At forty my young sons have grown and are gone,
But my man's beside me to see I don't mourn.
At fifty once more babies play round my knee,
Again we know children my loved one and me.
Dark days are upon me, my husband is dead,
I look at the future I shudder with dread,
For my young are all rearing young of their own,
And I think of the years and the love that I've known.
I'm an old woman now and nature is cruel—
'Tis her jest to make old age look like a fool.
The body it crumbles, grace and vigour depart,
There is now a stone where I once had a heart.
But inside this old carcass a young girl still dwells,
And now and again my battered heart swells.
I remember the joys I remember the pain,

And I'm loving and living life over again.
I think of the years all too few—gone too fast,
I accept the stark fact that nothing can last.
So open your eyes, nurses, open and see,
Not a crabbit old woman, look closer
—SEE ME! (Anon)

Pensive, pregnant pause in order here, I think.

We all know somebody that could have written that. Isn't it brilliant?
OK—that's enough!

Come back to me! Where am I? Oh yes, the first block of intensive
rehabilitation in the hospital.

I asked my brother, "Is my speech getting any clearer?" A pensive silence
was his immediate response, then "Yes . . . I don 't have to listen to you
quite so hard now . . . you're still boring though!" Thanks. Well, I was a
bit repetitive. Well I was a bit . . . get the drift? To overcome this annoying
snag, it was suggested that if I had a sneaking suspicion that I had told
them before, usually the thud of their forehead on the table when they
have fallen asleep again is a bit of a giveaway, I should stop and ask, "Have
I told you this before?" I should just really complicate and confuse the
issue. And why not? So, I was telling my brother my current favourite
joke:

"Why is . . . oh . . . have I told you before?" He narrowed his eyes, "I don't
know . . . go on . . .' " "Why is semen white and urine yellow?" He tutted . . .
"So the Irish man can tell whether he's comin' or goin' . . .

Yes! about forty times! Now, shut up!" I've probably told him since. Ha.
I must have told everybody forty times, I still remember it.

"Have I told you this before?" Now is that a helpful open question? or
what? I don't know. My brother said that each time I asked him, he
couldn't remember and so gave me the 'benefit of the doubt'. Just maybe

they hadn't been told and they didn't know, maybe it was something new and wow . . . nope! Could have been though! It has happened. They get the new news for a few weeks, then the old news again. In case they hadn't been told, or in case they'd forgotten the other thirty nine times that they had. Well, I had! Who's the fool? Them for inviting me to rabbit away—again!—or me for believing that this was the first time, every time and laughing all over again? I still do it.

My brother should greet me, "Hello . . . and yes, you've probably told me everything about everything." I start rabbiting away, as you do if given the 'floor space'. He interrupts, "You've told me . . ." My usual come-back, "Yes . . . but did I tell you about . . .?" Then homing in on some forgettable, irrelevant, petty detail and questioning him about it. He can't answer, of course, it's not that he hasn't heard it enough times or at all, it's that he can't remember every little thing I tell him. I then tell him everything, all over again. I woke him up, and we've sussed it now. When he says he's heard it before, he has to give me some details, so I believe him! proof! I too have this in order, 'yes . . . but . . .' re-opens floor space, and always works. I know that they have heard it then. Until next time . . . The really sad thing is that I know I do it!—with hind sight. What is the answer? To never speak at all, or for those around to be a little tolerant. I don't stumble about and repeat myself for effect. This is real, and I can do very little about it—if anything at all.

It's irritating, annoying, embarrassing, puzzling, boring? Well try my shoes on mate! Nobody has got a 'perfect' memory. I'm sorry! Good perhaps, but not infallible. Can you remember what you had for lunch two days ago? What you said to who? If you think about it, yes kinda, sometimes. A head injury exaggerates this natural and normal disability. The first sighting that I recall of Pathetic, I knew I knew him. Probably as he was walking to my bed grinning and looking directly at me—that was it. My wedding and engagement rings had vanished, so no clues there. "Who am I?" "You're a goldfish dear."

I was having a weird time those first few months after I returned to the UK. For example, I couldn't feel hot bath water on my legs. Had it always been? is it new? Dunno, just became aware of it that's all, looking like a ripe tomato from the 'waist' down couldn't really be missed. It didn't hurt, or make me sick, I just became aware of 'something else' to contend with. To this day, I do what I have to do in the bath, then I get out. I did buy myself a floating candle, to encourage mellow moments in a scented 'sauna' (the bath). My pubic hairs had grown back by this time, so using the candle gave images of 'forest fires' which put me off. But you were in the bath! With water! I hear you argue ... Yeah so? There's always a first time for everything, and whichever way you look at it I'm not the luckiest person on this planet. Why tempt fate? I don't really want to stay in the bath anyway. So, if you win a floating candle in a raffle, instead of a colour TV! erm, enjoy!

On my weekends home, if I was taken anywhere I had to go by 'chariot'. My chair had wheels that were tiny and I couldn't reach them! I therefore had to be pushed. The insurance companies would have piggy-backed me around as their bills for pranged cars became bankruptcy extortionate. If I'd have been steering ... the imagination runs riot! Out in the wheelchair, usually being pushed by mum, we'd pass people that my mum knew— some vaguely. After a while of being talked around and over (does she take sugar?), I'd start to get audibly grumpy. Then they'd remember that I was there and talk to me. Sometimes this attention was annoying, I'd firstly answer the 'kiddy talk', and be calm and patient with the 'Ahs'. I used to get really wound up, letting rip if, "I know exactly how you feel." was said to me in a sympathetic voice. Even more so if the person was stroking my arm with understanding. "No ... you don't." was my still quite rational reply. Then I would have lost it as I repeated "NO ... YOU DON'T." By now the record's stuck: "NO YOU DON'T!" stropping physically too and moving the chair alarmingly. My mum would usually interject, "Stop it or you'll end up on your nose!"

I knew of that radio programme, 'Does he take sugar?' I think I'm correct—in that it was a chat show investigating and discussing issues concerning disabilities. They had a blind guest who was supported by his wife. The DJ, apparently, on dishing out cups of tea, asked the wife, "Does he take sugar?" to which the wife replied, "Ask him." I understood—now. You can see it in people's eyes, they are embarrassed, they don't want to offend you, they don't know what to say or do, or they presume you are stupid. So talk to the 'pusher' it's much easier, and safe. I see it from the wheelchair now. It's bloody annoying. Miss Perfect here, I'm sure that I was as ignorant in my previous life. Having to repeat yourself over and over to be understood is annoying too. So, again, what to do?

My brother took me for walks—'cos it's good for you! fatty'. It may have been, but at the time it was not fun. It bloody hurt and it took me AGES to get ANYWHERE. As I over-compensate for my destroyed sense of balance, it gets too painful to proceed. My parents—still 'together'—lived in a village, not too far from a river, well, stream. My brother, fed up of pushing a fat whining lump around, and being limited to where we went (always the same flippin' place!), offered some brotherly advice, "Get rid of the chair, we've got nothing but time." Good point . . . so, off I jolly well crashed and wobbled on two sticks. Still went shopping in the chair, well it was good for carrying cumbersome things!

Rambling one day, as you do, in the country. My brother, a cyclist and a bit 'fit', offered to piggy-back me. One half of my brain was telling me off, "Wimp we've only been going half an hour! Wuss!" The other half was saying, "yeah! over mountains, into ravines and every step in the 'wild' countryside meant unravelling your foot from the under growth." My brain hadn't got to the, 'lift your feet' bit. It still hasn't. I couldn't jump up onto his back. After headbutting him a few times, we decided that me bouncing around trying to get onto his back, like a broken Zebedee in danger of wetting myself with laughter, maybe wasn't such a good idea after all. This is not difficult we can do this! We did! wow!

Once up, I couldn't stay up! No . . . I couldn't stay upright. Couldn't stay upright, hold on AND control my legs! I was a sniggering hump! He

RAN for a long time. Fit or what? I was getting cuddly—wheelchair shaped—then too! Totally in awe, I can't even imagine how he did that! It hasn't been tried since. Being piggy backed, not being a sniggering hump! I wonder? He's just read this, turned to look at me nodding, "Na."

I went to the local post office, which is five minutes walk away; where they'd seen me crumpled in the wheelchair when I first got back. The owners looked like toothpaste adverts, on my very grand, loud, solo, debut entrance. They didn't need to say anything. I wouldn't have heard anyway, I was too busy tutting and grumbling because it had taken me HALF an hour! But I was really flushed that I'D DONE IT! They'd be gobsmacked now, I've improved vastly.

When left alone in my parent's back garden, for any amount of time, I would be found weeding. In my parent's, the 'I'm not bothered—I'm not doing it', overgrown, very weedy garden. I could SEE I was making a difference. I was having some impact. I still do it—weeding that is. My mum has just moved into a new house. The garden was SO bad, a farmer friend sprayed it with industrial weed killer. It was so bad they've started growing back! bliss. I've visited, dressing appropriately for travelling, and every time it's, "I'll be really careful, I'll just pull up the big weeds for, five minutes whilst I have a cigarette . . ." EVERY time I get all carried away and end up grunging in the dirt after COUCH GRASS, it goes on forever and if you leave ANY of the root, it grows BACK!

This fetish reminds me of the time my brother was temping in a frozen food factory. First day, he was given the task of checking for, and removing, weirdo peas, which involved scanning a conveyer belt of cooked peas. After his long hard day, my mum prepared dinner for him, meat and two veg for the 'working boy'. One of the veg being . . . peas. Well, my brother drained of colour, went speechless, whilst gawping, wide eyed, at his full plate. What's wrong with him? He then started chanting, "Green peas . . . green peas!" Almost hysterical, he stopped and started laughing. Whilst he scanned the peas on his plate. He's not doing that job anymore.

Anyway, when visiting my mum, she would greet me with a change of clothes, which were hers so I always left them, gardened in, for her to take care of. Understandably, she got fed up of doing my muddy laundry in her new dump. So, bring a change of clothing, or go home on the bus looking and smelling like a vagrant! Note, 'don't weed, don't go in the garden—at all' weren't options. It would be a really good idea, if I took the same change of clothing with me. Bit by bit, my whole wardrobe's turning into 'gardening gear' because I can never remember what I wore the last time. I should be able to recognise the appropriate clothing—for obvious reasons—but at this time I was doing my own laundry, need I say more?

This incident took place in the first year—I was back at home, weeding, and I needed a wee. Instead of traipsing ALL that way, indoors and upstairs, my mum would run and get the bedpan. Brilliant idea! The wheelchair! and me were pushed into the garage. All I had to do was unfasten and pull my jeans down and lower myself onto the bedpan, put into position by my mum. It all started to go horribly wrong when I couldn't undo my forty two inch 'waisted' jeans, then I was desperate. My mum, flustering, fumbling and trying to help me unfasten my jeans, whilst stopping me from falling over, whilst juggling with the bedpan, whilst trying not to wet herself with laughter at a ridiculous image. Which helped me—not. I crashed, just in time, half on and off the bedpan. That was a one off, the garage was never attempted again. There was urine everywhere. Some in the bedpan too!

There was a time when my brother had been left to babysit. He went indoors and left me quite contented and absorbed. I was reaching for something that was on the floor. Stretching too far I crashed loudly into a hurt heap with the wheelchair. As my brother scooped me up, checking I was alright he was asking in a strained voice, "What WERE you doing? Mum's gonna KILL me!"

You have to bear with me—I write my memories down as they come to me. I am trying to keep an ordered structure. We jump to year two to three now . . .

Her new singles pad was awful, the person that had lived there before had removed all the skirting boards, and burnt them! The front room looked very creative and artistic? I don't THINK so . . . it looked stupid. Moreover, it was badly painted a horrid blue. I like blue, but this was beyond description. It was unpleasant. She was going to leave it, 'until other things got sorted!' Wrong! I opened some magnolia paint, that was 'cheap' and 'couldn't be resisted', and was lying around waiting to be used. Started daubing, my brother joined in, then my mum. Result: the front room is not blue and my dad put a skirting board on. My dad's good at DIY, my mum's crap and they still talk. They just cannot live together. So, it looks OK. Well, there are no carpets, and a coal fire. The handprints can be painted over! At least it's not blue!

When I first came home and all of us were in the same house—the family home—we got a cat (my idea). She was really gorgeous, slim and entirely black. Well, after a few months my mum and brother watched the results of her 'tarting' around being born. I missed it, because it was midweek so I was in hospital. So now we had three cats, my dad was ecstatic, having objected to Suki—the mother—in the first place. Like all baby animals, they were too cute and funny, naming them, dad suggested "Bloody thing."—for both! I named the sneaky tom 'Kez', the loud fat one was called 'Mo' by my brother—she was black with white patches that when spilling over onto the black looked like mohair. My mum gradually renamed her 'Daisy' as in, 'oops a . . .' She didn't know who she was, but she knew where the food was. Always first there and last to leave. Never too far away either. Suki, disappeared. Was she starving to death because her baby was eating all the food?

Time for them to be 'done'. Mum took them to the vets, where it was discovered they were both boys. Daisy? oh well. My mum insisted that "she, HE, was too pretty to be a boy." About a week later Kez got squashed on the road outside. My dad, heartbroken, tutted something about timing, and grumbled about needing a part for his bike. So two down, one to go. He was taken, by my mum, to her new place. Where he blew a TOTAL fuse to be let out. He visited occasionally and was finally seen in a carrier bag. The road outside my mum's leads to and from a motorway—it was really a matter of time.

I really looked forward to the weekends at home, nobody was ill (**skipped back to year one**). At the weekend my mum would take me to a local bingo hall. It was becoming a weekend thing. I went home, ate coconut cakes and played bingo. Bingo, in my experience is addictive. Not cheap, but addictive. I loved it. Once I got there, wheelchair and mum, I could do it all on my own. No training! We always had to sit at the front, it was the only place I could fit with the chair. I got an assortment of 'dabbers'. Different colours, my 'lucky' dabber was a different one each week! I could hold and use them, which meant I wasn't pushed out looking like a clown. We won sometimes, it will be the BIG one next week! Which we won't need because we'll have won the lottery! Sad thing is, my mum who was pandering to my whims, now calls me to see if I'm going? She's got her own dabbers now too! My dad came with us, his dabber is pink one week and red the next it's a bit dodgy. I don't know where he got it from and he calls now too.

Gadget Boy came to visit. My mum was happy to see her 'hero' again, and he showed her and my brother his new, expensive, path finding gadget. 'Essential' when four wheel driving in the desert, he logged in the coordinates for my parent's home. Meaning that wherever he was in the world he would be able to locate us! (damn). He took me for walks, pushed the chair around the countryside near my parent's house. Going down one lane I spied BLACKBERRIES! He stopped when I told him that I would like to pick some. I got out of the chair and fell over on the rough uneven grass. Undeterred and on the floor anyway, I crawled over to the brambles which were down a small rugged ditch. We left when we'd got enough and I was adequately shredded.

My parent's house was three bedroomed, my brother had a double futon taking up the floorspace in his bedroom. Looks nice, and you must get used to sleeping on them! It made sense that Gadget Boy and I slept in there. He was 'desperately in love with me'—note was. Lots of clumsy awkward fumbling as we were in bed. I don't know why, nor did I care, but nothing happened as it wouldn't play! Which to me said, YOU have LOST IT! What is left of you is far too repulsive.

We spoke with Giant Fairy (another friend) and arranged to go and visit. 'Arranged' in that Gadget Boy took me down to his house and Giant Fairy dumped me back at mine. All was well until bed time, when I had offers of sleeping on the settee with Gadget Boy or upstairs in bed with Giant Fairy, next to the toilet. Lots of uncoordinated fumbling again. Again nothing happened, as in again nothing happened! He fancied me in my previous life too. That confirms it, I'm an ugly goldfish. It got worse, when downstairs in the morning it was discovered that Gadget Boy had got up and gone, leaving a caustic explanatory note for me on the sofa.

Giant Fairy took me home saying 'he'd be in touch' on leaving. Tart! He went ex-directory and never spoke to me again. I know about the phone number as I tried to call him recently about this book. Not before, I wasn't that bothered. One of many.

Looking through my address book was a bit distressing, I had already lost touch with half the names in it. Some of the remaining names were of people I couldn't picture and didn't know how they fit into my life, if they still did. I had to go by feelings, if the name made me smile I informed them of this nightmare occurrence in my life. Giant Fairy was one of these who was on business near us and so called in to visit, I'd forgotten how tall he is. Over six and a half feet. I slept in my brother's futon with him and absolutely nothing happened—again.

A few wrote and sent photographs of their kids; all my school friends have moved on. The correspondence just petered off, but the initial thoughts were appreciated. One commented, "God you've had it rough—it's not fair!" One of the names was of somebody I went out with as a teenager. I should have stayed with him! He is still an absolute star and came to see me in the unit. "You only ring me when you've had an accident!" He was around the last time too; his wife was a little dubious of me even though she didn't know me and hadn't met me. He stopped contact too, having a young family now.

CHAPTER THREE

uring the second year of recovery, Gillian spent time in a rehabilitation unit, followed by a period in a semi-independent bungalow attached to the unit. Subsequently, she moved into accommodation known as 'Near Reach'. Unfortunately, this did not meet her needs and she returned to the bungalow before moving into her current flat.

The Second Year

A rehabilitation centre for the aftermath of head injuries is not a hospital so the inmates aren't patients, they are clients. One lunch time there was a new cook, the full time cook was off sick. The menu said, 'Cheesy Pasta Bake'. Yum, one of my favourites. Got my meal and sat with the unit manager. We both, prodding and moving the pasta about, small talked (whilst rescuing the pasta from the sea of orange grease on which it was floating!). Yes it was pasta, yes it was baked, yes it was cheesy. Distracted by the crash of a knife and fork, I saw that this delicacy had been abandoned by our mentor. "I'm not hungry!" he said, convincingly. Looked down at my bobbing shells—"Coward." I said convinced. Very temporary cook, she was never seen again—made our normal cook look good though.

Another lunch, I was sitting with a fellow client who was also shell-shocked by the calm, the quiet. It was an abnormal situation. Nothing was happening? We thought too soon, raised voices grabbed my attention just in time to see the action. A physically large client punched a lanky client so hard he lifted him off his feet! Excellent! The recipient of this thump suffered so badly with his epilepsy that his face was always covered in cuts, scratches and bruises. He had probably said something to deserve it. Turning to the other client, shrugging, I commented, "Something ALWAYS happens here EVERY meal time!" Just as I finished the sentence a female client verbally erupted whilst continually and viciously kicking a male client under the table. I giggled excitedly "SEE!" Perfect timing. Excellent! you took less notice of the food. If we'd had cheesy pasta every other day, none of us would have noticed. And we probably did!

My meals and drinks had to be carried to my table for me. I just had to get myself to the same place. I still cannot carry cups and liquids; by the time I get to my destination my vessel is almost empty. It goes all over my new carpet and kitchen floor which will be trodden and slipped in later. My very first room at the Unit was next door to the staff room. I was female and vulnerable. One day a male client just sauntered into my bedroom! Woah! If he hadn't left on three . . . I informed him, the Piper Haven (an internal alarm) would be pulled. (Hand poised threateningly by the pull cord). "I'm not doing anything! I'm not touching you!" was his reaction. "Three!" He left, miffed.

Another client prone to frequent loud outbursts always flattened any reasoning with an irate, "I couldn't give a turquoise toss!" There is NO answer! She gave me a welcome gift, a fluffy toy. A few days later I was the sounding board for one of her turquoise toss tantrums and she took it off me! Thought she'd come to talk.

For each working day you have a timetable, of 'planned activities', detailed on Monday morning so you know what you are doing for the rest of the week. Where you are supposed to be, when and why? Each morning after breakfast your daily routine was confirmed and you are notified of any changes. This was called 'orientation'. At one such session there was a new boy sitting with a blank timetable in front of him. He asked what it was for? I tried to tell him, the 'helper' interrupted, "Stop interrupting!" "He hasn't got a clue what's going on, I was trying to explain." I counteracted defensively. A little while later he asked again, "What are these for? What do you do with them?" Silence. Started trying to explain again.

The same 'helper' voice raised, "Shut up! Stop interrupting!" Pointed out that the new guy was just filling space. I was trying to fill him in. Believe this!—with the back of her hand on her forehead she cried, "I don't know what I'm doing here!" (We were paying her wages because of our injuries). Bloody prima donna daft bag. "Neither do I." I answered helpfully, got up and left. Thought I'd get into loads of trouble for this, nothing was said by anybody—at all. Gutted. Be—quiet—please. I should have asked her which word was difficult?

There was one other client for orientation. On my timetable was shopping, his was blank. Told him to ask somebody if he could come with me. The same 'helper' retaliated, "No, he can't he's got problems!" Then she left. I glanced over saying, "You can't, YOU'VE got problems!" We laughed. She jumped back from nowhere to within inches from my face and spat, "I heard that! He's got problems that I need to discuss!" She turned away and left again! This really shook and disturbed me visibly, which really upset the other client. Lovely guy.

One of the sessions was an assertive class. Somebody always freaks verbally and drags half the class into it, we'd get side-tracked mentally and then couldn't remember what had just been said, about what. They were a bit of a bore really, same same . . . the only interesting bits were the scenes. I wasn't there when this next incident happened—wish that I had been. A client, friend, stood up excusing herself—and was asked where she was going? "Out." was the reply. She was told to sit down as she had to stay, it was an important class. I can imagine . . . what started out to be important sessions get sidetracked and interrupted, usually by the same people. "No, I'm leaving." she said "How was that for assertive?" she questioned, and left. Excellent! If I'd had the nerve.

An activity had been arranged, a trip to Granada Studios where Coronation Street is made. A request by a client who was an avid fan. She REALLY wanted to go. There was a space and a helper had asked if I could go as a 'special treat', even though I didn't really want to and hadn't asked. Yes! I could go! I went because I was made to feel it was a special privilege and that people had gone out of their way to accommodate me. Also, why not? Two other clients were in the car, one wheelchair bound, the other making up numbers too. We were driven all the way to Manchester. Awful, I get bored and impatient very quickly. Very long jaunts I can handle, just go to sleep. Easy.

My dad commented, "You were like that when you were little!" He then told me family trips always began, "We've just set off!" then "We're nearer than we were!" and, "We're nearly there!" from this point this was the answer to my incessant "We nearly there yet?" That bugs me to this day, 'we're nearly there' means we're miles away and it's going to be ages. On this journey it was disclosed that we had to pay the entry fee for ourselves and the helper. It wasn't so bad, there were three of us! We got completely lost, with three really patient passengers, eventually reaching our destination. The studios were closed to the public on Mondays. It was Monday. The client that requested this was heartbroken. I was annoyed we'd have had to pay for the helper. I hadn't wanted to go in the first place! We all went to Harry Ramsdens, my suggestion; credit to me, and it was very nice. Salvaged something out of this farce. I let it be known, my disappointment, disgust and dismay by such thoughtless inadequacy. Scoring major brownie points on the popularity scales. Went on, it only needed a phone call, then such a costly waste of a day could have been avoided. AND it would have cost ME loads had it been open.

There was one client who pointed out (on a daily basis), "This place is a fuckin' 'ole!" in a Geordie accent. We understood this; sadly, there were days that he had to be agreed with. The food (as mentioned), in my opinion was lacking any imagination. The sandwich days were bad. There were 'treat' days, when you could order take-away food and you got two pounds fifty towards your order. Any surplus you had to pay. Encouraged and time-tabled self catering was the same deal!

There were sixteen clients in the Unit, so at one thousand pounds a week, per client, that is sixteen thousand pounds every week. I know there are overheads . . . but really . . . I was having a particularly grim time as my benefits hadn't been sorted and I was getting intermittent unpleasant phone calls from Pathetic. Why he bothered when they were 'costing a fortune' and really rocking my boat, I don't know.

Once there were about seven of us waiting in a room for a planned session to begin. The helper was late. For the first five minutes it was peaceful; for the next five, ripples were appearing, after ten minutes there were four of them full flow 'turquoise tossing'. Another five minutes when it was starting to get nasty, the helper emerged, tutted, sat down, looked at her watch, tutted again and said, "Sit down and shut up." Off I went, collecting brownie points again, this time my point was, considering that she was fifteen minutes late she was out of order with her tutting attitude as she entered a battle zone. Being staff in a brain injury rehabilitation centre, one would have expected a little more tolerance if not understanding. It wasn't a new scenario, probably not different people either. Surely an apology for her tardiness, not necessarily a reason, would have been reasonable to hope for—well at least civil. Instead of making us feel that our short fuses and general lack of self control were the cause.

My swimming was encouraged, so I would go again, although not very happy about it. I didn't need help getting changed this time, good start. A grab-railed ramp led into the water. So far ... in my mind, I was ably proficient. In my body—not at all smooth, controlled, safe or fun. 'But you didn't drown!' I was told. Oh yeah! ... My knees ached, badly enough to stop me from swimming. 'Unfit' explained this snag away. They did this scheme whereby all your lengths are counted up each week towards a recognition goal. Got into this and was a gold medallist or would have been had my knees not stopped me. Told the physiotherapist (who is now selling knickers on a market stall), who gave me a stretchy strip of tube bandage. Which did not work at all.

It was swimming day and I 'came on', (yes!), but had a horrendous headache too. Wobbled to the staff room to tell them, and therefore cancel any arrangements. A member of staff responded, "You do that all the time, let everybody down!" It had been done once and I had told them hours before the expedition. PMT? Was a bit ruffled by this response, you bag! Don't think that swimming was continued.

Started signing classes, I'm still doing it! Each hearing person should know hello, goodbye, sorry and thank you, and how to swear! in sign language. It's interesting; the tutor was deaf and one coffee break she was telling us that her son, also deaf, did a sign she didn't recognise. He wouldn't tell her at first, she persisted, intrigued now that she didn't totally understand his signing. Eventually he had to finger spell it. It meant 'fuck off'—well she did ask. When we came out of this 'break' we knew five swearing signs, which I still remember!

My lift back from class was totally unreliable; the excuses were ridiculous. Even more so when you've been stood outside waiting for nearly half an hour. They 'thought' it ended at a different time! I had been going to this class for months, on the same day at the same time each week AND my arrangements were confirmed in 'orientation' too (the Unit's method of telling us our weekly programme), so I know where I'm going and they know where I am. Eventually, taxis were arranged and I had to pay for them.

Taxis . . . I could write a book! I ordered a taxi when living on my own in year three, a week in advance for a hospital appointment. An appointment that had been made months ago with the kidney guy (specialist). So I explained that it was important and that I had difficulty with mobility; my appointment is at twenty past nine, I said, repeating, "I'm disabled and it's a hospital appointment." They would be there at ten past nine then, they said (The hospital is just round the corner by car, but a long way by foot). At nine I was ready and waiting on the front step. At five past I came back in and telephoned, asking were they coming? It's important a hospital appointment! "Yes, yes . . . delays . . . traffic . . ." Went back out. Back in at nine fifteen and called again. "He's there now!" he yelled. I apologised for calling. Fumbled in my effort to get out quickly already being late and not wanting to keep the taxi waiting. Got back outside, went back in a few minutes later. Telephoned again,

"No he's not! I'm late for my appointment now where is he?" He replied exasperated, "I don't know." and there was nothing he could do, "Did I understand?" I called the hospital in tears telling them I couldn't get a taxi. I'd have to walk and I was already half an hour late. This specialist comes to this hospital once a week and I'd been queueing for months. Don't worry, they said, just come when you can. Just closing the door and the taxi pulled up. On the way to the hospital he was moaning, took him half an hour . . . traffic . . . roadworks. I noted that he hadn't got a radio and asked why? His boss was, "Too tight!" he answered. I was annoyed. When he'd hollered, "He's there now!" and I'd apologised for calling again—he was lying.

We got there and it was further than I thought, so I was duly concerned about getting home. Therefore asked him for a business card so I could call when I was ready. The fare was three pounds, I gave him a ten pound note. He handed me the change, lots of coins. I vaguely checked them as I was over half an hour late now. They looked wrong. Opened my purse again. Five pound coins, two fifty pences and three twenty pence pieces. He'd just had to call at a cashpoint for me to get some money, "Otherwise I can't pay!" So ten pounds was all I'd had. Gosh, adding insult to injury he'd short changed me. Held the change out in my hand to show him, and told him this. Forty pence I chipped back. It was the principle, not the money. Had he not whined all the way when I was so cross, I would have tipped him—maybe! He fumbled around tutting and heaving then gave me a card. I kept my hand out and raised my eyebrows. He turned and fumbled some more tutting and huffing. I got out, I really couldn't be bothered or be any later than I already was. So he got a forty pence tip!

Hospital staff called a taxi for my return journey, it would be ten minutes. It was, and the fare was two pounds. Telling the driver of the earlier taxi incident he only commented, that he was, "not surprised!" Excellent! now he tells me!

Months ago. Evening school. The taxi dropped me off and I told them to pick me up at the same spot at nine o'clock, as I had difficulty with my mobility. Twenty past nine, no taxi. My friend was still with me and had to give me a lift home. Rang the taxi firm when I got back, asking where were they? Answer—they were waiting at the other side of college. Different driver. If my friend hadn't been there I would have been stuck . . . I was so cross that I said I wouldn't be using them again. So? . . . was the attitude.

One of the staff at the Unit was a member of a local working men's club which did bingo every week. It was great, a night out, different faces, a drink and bingo. Always sat with the same little crowd, as you do. At morning orientation I had to tell them to stop verifying the bingo out loud, and thereby announcing to everybody that was where I was going and what I was doing. I was under instructions not to idly chat about the club as it was this member of staff's club, for 'normal' guys, but it was alright for me to go as I wasn't prone to freaking out. I liked the club, the people and understood, so didn't say anything. It was made general knowledge every week, and every week the same client would casually wander in my direction and ask where I was going and why? At first I would happily tell her of my plans, then I'd get quizzed about the club, leading onto the searching why did I go? and not her? The tempest peaking with the 'she didn't do anything and she didn't go anywhere' tantrums. By now, the situation was out of control. This routine was getting tedious, so I rudely played deaf and dumb for a little while. They stopped announcing, she stopped getting wound up and therefore grilling me, I kept going. After a while a male client was allowed to come with me to the bingo at the working man's club, it was good for him and for lots of reasons it was our secret. He had been beaten up and he wasn't a young man, his confidence had taken a real hammering. He was a lovely chap, the one who had 'problems', we always shared our winnings. Well mine! He never won!

In the bedroom, there was an en-suite bathroom that didn't have a bath, just a shower in the corner and onto a slip proof textured floor. Hadn't had a shower yet. Did I want a bath chair? they asked. Don't know, was my answer. "You'd better take it, you'll slip, fall and hurt yourself!" was the persuasive argument. "But I might not." was mine. I wouldn't take the chair saying, "You never know until you try!" Off we went to put our money where our mouth was. I didn't fall over, but it's very hard having a shower with one hand whilst slipping and continually retrieving dropped essentials trying not to break anything (all one-handed as the other one is being permanently occupied keeping your backside off the treacherous floor). Dropping the flannel, the soap, the shampoo, flannel, soap, soap, flannel . . . Had to get this resolved, or go mad and resign to the chair. Got it! Just wash your hair, and work your way down! Not ideal, but I didn't smell and my hair was clean.

Dabbling with arty things again, an inspiration accompanied with huge gestures and colourful mess. The art cupboard was very basic and incredibly lacking. On asking if they had ANYTHING else, (crayons are fine but we're not children), I was told to take a look in the art cupboard. Disappointingly, there was little else, but had a great time sorting and ordering what there was. Luckily everybody understood the hieroglyphics for crayon. Nobody looked at it any way. Whilst in there, loads of jigsaws were spied. Liking jigsaws, I asked a member of staff why they were locked away (The room was also used for staff coats and bags hence out of bounds). "You only had to ask." was the answer. Oh yeah right . . . out of sight out of mind! Wouldn't it be a good idea if they were stored in the sitting room so that they can be seen and used? Well it made sense to me. This couldn't be done as the pieces would get lost? Took a few whilst there and did them in my room, probably losing a few bits! as you do!

How is it WHEN you live alone, you do your own laundry, only your clothing, yet you ALWAYS have a spare sock. I've got a drawer full of odd socks, the partners are around . . . actually there are probably some pairs in there now. I ought to look. When we all get to heaven we will be surrounded by our lost socks, lighters and keys. How was that for a smooth change of topic?

Laundry was on my timetable, sorted them in my linen basket into dark and light washes. Got my full basket to the laundry room with great difficulty. All two machines were in use, we had all been time-tabled laundry at the same time. Left the basket in the queue with a named label, with the intention of returning later to complete the task. Returned later and my laundry was in the dryer. A member of staff had done it for me. Nicely. Pulled a new sweater, worn once, from the dryer (a gift from Pathetic the Christmas before), a cream sweater stained with big ugly streaks of grey. Held it out straight wailing, "Look at my jumper! No! Look at my jumper!" The onlooking 'helper' chastised, "Gillian you're freaking about nothing!" Was silenced, it was only a jumper. Thinking about it later, when my mum had taken it to save it, yes it was only a jumper, but it was MY jumper. A new sweater that could have suffered the same fate at my hands but, it didn't. Would have liked to see her reaction had I done this to a new sweater of hers then insinuated that she was out of order being a bit peeved. Having told people, as I was upset, as well as a bit disturbed by her reaction, when the next time-tabled 'laundry' session happened, the same helper sneered, "But of course you don't WANT any help do you, you want to do it all on your own." Bag! I'd gone off her.

Another vulnerable female arrived, so I was moved to another room. Opposite a man who was so severely disabled by his head injury that he had bars around his bed to prevent him from falling out. I know this as it was impossible for me to sleep until he did—normally in the early hours. To be abruptly jolted into consciousness by a loud intrusive serenade, his name being shouted by him continually, with rattling bed bars as accompaniment. I was becoming a zombie, falling asleep in the afternoons, exhausted, before I entered his room, finding out he wasn't in pain and then punching him saying, "You've got something to shout about now!" I was moved, again, my third room in the unit.

I did try to mingle with the other clients during the evening when nothing was time-tabled. There were too many verbal distractions in the TV room, some clients you just couldn't hold a conversation with, and there was little else to do. Trivial pursuit was boring when the helpers kept winning so I agreed to play Monopoly with another client. He went round the board once and then bought EVERYTHING that he landed on. I was completely wiped out by the tenth round. I agreed to play him another time, and he did exactly the same thing—it's very boring. I don't really think it's a game for two players!

I tried staying at the unit for a weekend one time, and went home every other. The first time I caught a train alone was a visit home one weekend. My parents couldn't, for some reason, pick me up on the Friday night. Calm down, they would collect me the next day—Saturday. I assured them that I could do this; said I would have emergency numbers; said that I wouldn't try and carry more than my toothbrush; said I would call them later with the train time and rang off indignantly. All I was doing was catching a train, not thinking about the trek any more. I was given a lift to the station—so far so good. Found out which platform I needed and set off, the train was in and I tried to move faster. I was inches from the train, and I watched it pull off. I almost fell onto the lines and was helped by a British Rail employee who calmed me down and got me to a train that was leaving soon. It went near to where I wanted to be, but involved a change. Excellent. I was getting off this train and the doors closed, my bag was still on the train. Not a big deal you would think but the bag handles were on my shoulder, the bag was still on the train and I couldn't open the doors. I couldn't try as I was focussed on staying upright. One of the guards noticed my dilemma and assisted. My first journey alone and I'd missed the train and almost got dragged to Glasgow on the alternative. I was incredibly jubilant when I saw my parents, getting back would have to be easier—there was only one train to catch and my parents would ensure that I didn't miss it.

I was gradually assessed and as a result moved into a bungalow attached to the unit. Alone, to fend for myself. They were only round the corner but it was a huge effort to go round. My motivation is still almost non-existent, exaggerated by my physical disabilities. I often spent days totally alone—partially by choice. Started writing a lot, letters, poems and lists.

MAYBE (1994)

It seems like only yesterday . . .
What day is it ? Oh yes . . . today.
The day is long and hard to fill,
Maybe I should take a pill,
One that makes pain disappear
Or one that makes me smile from ear to ear!
I would, if I could, I should—I WOULD! if I could . . .
Maybe.

TIME (loads) (May 1994)

Time on my own, my own space.
Time to reflect, pose and ponder,
Time to think.
To think of things never questioned before,
To think . . .
Time, tick, tick.
Behind four walls is my place,
To make a mess if I choose,
To smoke as much as I want
I'm alright! I'm OK! I'm NORMAL!
What is normal?
Am I being unfair? I wonder,
Am I being intolerant petty?
Are they really as awful as they seem?
Or is it me?
She thinks—maybe.
Self denial creeps in again,
It's been nearly a year . . .
So soon, a year already?
One day I'll come to terms with this,
One day . . . maybe . . . tick, tick

DYH (April 1995—June 1996)

"I couldn't give a turquoise toss!"
"It is disgusting!"
Time on my own—
Time is the great healer.
Melodramatic time . . . "shut your hole you stupid cow!"
Time . . .
How much do I need?
How much do I want?
Time to think . . . tick, tick,
Memories, distractions,
"This fuckin' ole!"
Rehabilitation : the gradual erosion of remaining sanity.
How much time do you get for murder?
Tick, tick . . . KABOOM.

WHAT . . . . . . May 1996.

. . . . . . are you thinking ?
. . . . are you feeling ?
. . . . are you doing ?
. . . . . . do you want ?
Ask the questions, be polite.
Who gives a damn . . . I know I'm right

WHO DARES. June 1996.

Skip across the lily pads,
. . . NAY DANCE!
Trust yourself.
Don't count on anybody—there is only
really you,
On your own.

So, where are those lily pads?

June 1997

At least where is the ******* pond ?

You don't really have to be a literature graduate to read between the lines of these poems. You would guess that frustration played a very large role here since I mention 'time' often. Time, clocks and bombs. Psychiatry graduates would have fun affixing labels, and reasoning with this!

I was going to visit Pathetic—my first visit to him (I had to take my mum because I couldn't travel alone), for my third wedding anniversary. It was important to me, I'd missed my second because of the accident. Since I was married and making up lost time it was presumed that rude stuff would be occurring. (A message to him from me—By the way, I lied). At the time, just the initial steps were all that I needed. Actions, not words, which said 'you are still OK, Gill'. I'm still gobsmacked that I did this. For some reason—unknown to me—I told Pathetic about the incidents with the Giant Fairy and Gadget Boy. I don't think he was very happy. Though he didn't show it at the time.

If I got pregnant, it was only a good idea in that I'd have a big fat stomach to bounce off when I fell over. A form of contraceptive was needed. As I'd been taking the combined pill previously, they put me on the mini pill for a while. Which you have to take at the same time, give or take a few hours, every day, or you have a period. After my tenth period that month when I was becoming anaemic, it was decided that maybe that's not the way. We are talking babies and stuff here. Back to the Doctor, this time for an injection of something that confuses ovaries so much that you are a baby-free zone for three months. That's it, you don't have to do anything else. Don't know why I didn't just have this in the first place.

In the bungalow leading a normal life with a head injury (I can't think of a witty sarcastic remark here). Probably as it's not that funny, means that fending for yourself you have to plan, budget for and purchase your own groceries or have nothing to eat. Well that's the theory I presume. I just bought what I liked and fancied, nobody checked. As I don't drive I had to be taken. They came in with me telling me what I should be buying. "I don't like it . . ." worked sometimes. Other times I'd go with the flow and choose something healthy and green. Throwing it away a few days later, when I noticed it was growing legs or going furry. With a fully laden trolley, we headed for the car. Struggled with the trolley, that had the usual stiff wonky wheels, to where I thought the car was. Must have forgotten, I thought, when it couldn't be seen. Turning to locate the driver hoping that it was in this general direction. She was looking over her shoulders with a puzzled frown, "Did we park it here?" she asked me. It had been stolen we eventually realized. Which meant the transport situation, as though it wasn't bad enough already, got worse. I started being dropped off at the supermarket to shop alone. Didn't listen to them anyway, so I was quite happy about this. All hunky dorey, until I was getting cold. It wasn't until nearly half an hour of waiting for my lift that I went back inside and rang the Unit demanding, "Where are you? I'm freezing!" "Who is this?" they answered then, "Where are you?" They had forgotten me. This inadequacy emphasises how I felt in the bungalow, 'out of sight, out of mind'.

As I'd enquired about my driving, an assessment had been arranged at an appropriate driving school in Derby. I was taken along by the job coach/ vocational manager. Firstly my breaking power and reaction speeds were measured, they must have been adequate as I was let onto a real road in a real car. The car was an automatic so that I didn't have to think about too much. Easy! Well I knew what I was meant to be doing, in theory. In practice, I was a boy racer or a kangaroo. I was alright until the car in front of me braked, then I'd get distracted by the red lights and knew that I should be doing something but couldn't remember what to do, in time. The outcome being that the instructor had to keep correcting my steering, otherwise we'd have ended up in every front garden in Derby. It was when the report on my driving was handed to me that my fears were confirmed, I was not safe to be let out on the road again. It was at this point that I broke down and was incredibly upset, the job coach approached me and just touched my arm. No words could console me.

Pathetic rang, I wasn't there and didn't get the message. Setting our next conversation off to a good start, I went straight for the jugular accusing, "Why didn't you call?" Why didn't you call again then, later? or the next day? He was too busy, 'Work n' stuff'. What everyday, all day? They don't have phones in his office either? Completely devastated by his indifference and obvious boredom on the phone, whilst strangely not bothered. He wasn't there, in any way.

I invited my mum and brother round to the bungalow for dinner. Went totally OTT, as usual, got the napkins and everything. Three courses, that's the cooking done for the week. Living alone and being lazy, I love convenience foods. The main dish was moussaka, which I haven't done before. Or since! The recipe called for 'sliced turnip'. The only chopping knife in the bungalow had a blade two inches long. When the kitchen and turnip were bright red and I had trimmed all my nails (eventually, my nails all gone), it was decided that perhaps a little help was needed. Went into the unit and asked, explaining why. Half an hour later the handy man was passing my window and waved, I answered gesturing for him to come in. (He already knew me because when he'd just started the job, I laughed: "Well this job will be different!"). I handed him the red turnip and penknife saying, "Told you this job would be different!" Having plasters put on my fingers in the unit, I asked for a chopping knife with a blade that cut properly and questioning why the 'knife' in the bungalow was so crap. "To curb suicidal tendencies." Like I should have known. I told them that if you're going to commit suicide, you're going to do it however big your knife is and the one in the bungalow was already dangerous (displaying my hands). No new knife was provided whilst I was there. Maybe the next client didn't like moussaka! Alcohol was prohibited and I'd got vodka stashed all over the place and was sneakily drinking it in coffee to avoid detection. I drink a lot of coffee, I should never be asleep. I was falling all over the place, but not breaking any thing so it was OK. I woke up one morning with an intensely severe hangover. Oops! At four in the afternoon I could not believe how horrendous I still felt, went back to bed, having done— nothing. This sad practice ended there. Starting again when I moved onto the next step of rehabilitation— 'Near Reach'. You live in a house with another client and a member of staff. Two helpers alternating day and night. Like student days, and off we happily bounded. The other client was male, and I was told I'd like him as, "He's got a degree!" The other client watched only the news and quiz programmes on television, all day, every day. The homely touch being that smoking was banned in the front room, not that I wanted to watch TV. However, smoking was allowed in the dining room. Odd. I would often sit on the grass in the back garden, smoking, alone and occasionally drawing. The weather was nice in those days. I drew plans of the back garden and indicated how it would be changed if I had anything to do with it. Putting in a BBQ, table and chairs, patio . . . I didn't and so these sketches were never seen by anybody. I have no idea whether or not they have been binned . . . I can't remember what the garden looked like either, before or 'after'.

On a venture outdoors, I bought a crunchy lemon meringue pie mix to make later. It's lemon meringue on a biscuit base—like cheesecake— they are really, really nice. A support worker, Mr 'Withit' (read on to see why I call him this), had brought one of my friends over to see me. 'Withit' volunteered to help me make the pie. So we started. The mix has three packets. One obviously being the biscuit base another the lemon, the third the meringue—alright. You have to split one egg, the yolk going in the lemon filling and the white in the meringue. I thought that this was pretty obvious! No, Mr Withit got them the wrong way round! so we had a watery lemon bit and a flat yellow meringue. He saved the day by putting slices of banana on the top, to cover and hide the mess. It was like latex, the biscuit base was the only bit that was edible!

Mr Withit re-entered my life in year five, and this book stops at the end of year four. Here's a message for him, 'Think on—you owe me a lemon meringue!'

I had my own television in my bedroom with the still illegal vodka stashed in my knicker drawer, my suitcase and my laundry bin. Trying not to be ignorant, continually sitting in solitude in my room, scrabble was the answer! No, it wasn't. "That's the best I can do I'm afraid." he exclaimed before taking every single turn. One word he used was 'it', another, 'zodiac'. Completely wiping him out was becoming a chore, it was abandoned. Miss Patience here being in danger of stabbing him!

Every day I was made aware that his degree wasn't one subject, it was two combined and that he had been the editor of his student newsletter. Interesting, the first ten or so times. Even the way he ate got on my nerves. Back to the vodka—my secret. Excusing myself, I'd go into my den get faced and fall over. They were attempting to get me into routines. I was doing OK on my own.

The three of us went on a shopping expedition and were outside the supermarket. I didn't want to go in saying I wanted to look around—I wouldn't/couldn't go far. I'd got to go into the supermarket with them! Why? I queried. Reiterating, I couldn't go far ... If I didn't do as she said, we were going home! I was ruining it for everybody, I was being selfish, and she was going to tell somebody that I was disruptive, argumentative and I wouldn't do what she said! Ooooo! Unhappily trudged around the supermarket, where the other client told anybody and everybody that he was vegetarian. The climax, for me, came one morning. The helper appeared and poignantly put my timetable in front of me. The other client had finished eating and had gone to watch the news. "What are you doing?" she demanded. Looked at my cigarette, with raised eyebrows, "Having a shower." She didn't laugh. She replied, jabbing at the timetable, "TEN O' CLOCK—LAUNDRY!" Repeating this in case I didn't understand or was deaf (?) I'd got four pairs of socks in my laundry but I'd set the machine going if it made her happy was my response. A

GILLIAN MK 2

personality clash I was told. Call me pedantic, but don't you have to HAVE a personality first? The other client liked her.

The other helper would play scrabble with me, and cards. I showed her an addictive patience card game, she moaned weeks later that she still hadn't done it! Showed her another card game, where the winner legally (it's in the rules!), calls the loser a "Shithead!"—that's the name of the game. It's a bit disheartening being called this for an hour I suppose. I liked this game.

At my next review, where your (monitored) progress is discussed and the next stage is planned, I was totally gobsmacked when I received the write-up, "Gillian is drinking upstairs." Some goddamn secret, but the absconding upstairs routine followed shortly by appropriate crashes in the bathroom was a bit of a giveaway. Being heavily bruised the next morning confirmed suspicions. I was dreadfully unhappy there. The most unhappy I recall being throughout all of this.

My mum was stuck between a rock and a hard place. She was watching me crumble, and was really troubled by the drinking. But where else could I be? What to do for the best?

The bungalow at the unit happened to be empty, so I moved back. A sad time. It was decided that 'Near Reach' perhaps wasn't the right approach—for me. I wasn't grateful (verbally and continually) and happy enough and I wouldn't be told—anything. The 'job coach' came to see me. It was obvious I wasn't ready to go back to teaching. If anybody commented at this time, "Oh, you were a teacher?" I would foam at the mouth and spit "AM a teacher. Am." They did say "Were." I take things that are said very literally. I understand the English language, don't say it if you don't mean it.

In the bungalow there was an umbrella plant that I had bought for a previous occupier as a house warming gift. When he moved on to his own place, he either left it on purpose or forgot to take it. Whatever, I paid for it and it's now taking over my kitchen. When I moved to my own place I went to see him at his. He doesn't allow smoking in his house so his support worker joined me outside in the back garden. It was gloriously sunny and we were looking around and chatting, pulling up the odd weed. Which got bigger! The person I'd come to see, came outside to see where we were? He eventually half hearted joined in. The garden looked completely different when we stopped. I was flushed, he wasn't bothered. This was a friendship involving lots of mutual visiting. At the end of that day he said and did things that were too odd for me to deal with. The friendship petered out, but I'm always really happy to see him.

When I left to start life in my new shell, one of the helpers at the Unit, who I had a soft spot for, said that he came to this area often and would call in for coffee and a chat. The next time I saw him was on the street outside, he had brought a client shopping. I reminded him of his verbal commitment then added sarcastically that his coffee had gone cold— and evaporated! He apologised and laughed saying that he would come round soon. The next time I saw him was at the Unit when I visited, regarding the newsletter. I just raised my eyebrows and said, "Hi!" I think he's a bit of a berk now. Working with 'us' he should really be aware that if things are remembered they are important and taken literally; this quite normal response is exaggerated in people with head injuries. Remembering what was said is quite an achievement; thinking round the corners is too difficult when you've got to walk and breath.

Volunteer work was suggested to kill time, get me out of the bungalow, meet people, a routine, work mode . . . OK I'll go. A charity shop was decided upon. I was actually really looking forward to seeing the clothes and stuff that comes in and what happens to it. Oh yeah and meeting the people, getting out, routines . . . Well, bought some pictures, got an excellent silk shirt, was having a fab time.

One of the helpers had the till key fastened to her special work tunic, so that only she could use it. I wasn't allowed, and so I asked why, because

I wasn't intending to rob the till. For a start, one is lacking stealth, light footedness and speed. I knew how to work a till too! The answer, "You might make a mistake, then where would we be?" There isn't a sarcasm-free answer, and I couldn't think of anything else. So I just didn't touch the till. Was getting to know the regulars and met some of the other staff's families. It's amazing what items are 'one man's meat and another man's poison'. I love sorting and ordering things—making a visible impact. This faculty has always been important to me. Even if I am clumsily making a huge mess (usually for somebody else to clear up while thanking me for my help)—which I did, assisting in the charity shop. Always bashing, bumping and banging things and people, with one or both sticks; well it was that or fall over. (Is it me?—don't some of these women that volunteer at charity shop get on your nerves? Those with the snooty 'holier than thou' attitudes and if it wasn't for them the shop would collapse. Almost an attitude). My destroyed sense of balance means that I can't stand on one foot long enough to stride and step over things. When out and about I'd mentally 'log' a puddle or dog doings, and then walk straight through it!

Back at the unit pointlessly trying to locate information on the 'client's notice board', a bit silly really. There was no order at all, it was a mish-mash of kaleidoscopic paper. So bad that you got distracted totally and forgot why you were there. If the information was located it would be out of date. Irrelevance was masking important notices. The fire drill being amongst all of this crap—somewhere. I got the staff to let me into the 'art' cupboard, having told them I was going to orderly arrange the display. Didn't listen to any negativity, I just got on with it, saying that nothing useful would be thrown away and they could check the garbage (not waiting for written authority and approval). Those 'upstairs' probably didn't know there was a notice board, you couldn't see it. This is how I knew there was a fire drill, by completely stripping the board! When re-vamped, the board looked good. It was easy to read, find the information you needed and you could see where to go to make sure you weren't burnt. You could find out what was on at the theatres and cinemas now—today—and if you were desperate enough—when meal times were. If you could smell cooking, it was meal time, and probably cheesy pasta bake, and if you couldn't it was probably sandwich day. The presence of this notice wasn't essential, because if you could hear a commotion in the dining room, it was meal time.

Somebody was knocking on the front room window of the bungalow, to get my attention. On looking up, a grinning face indicated that he was coming in, and there he was again—the front door wasn't locked and this was the same client who was the reason my bedroom door was always locked when I was in the unit. As a result of his injury he is on a constant ego trip; if you're female, you fancy him. It's as simple as that. There's nothing wrong with being so confident, unless it means you are getting slapped by jealous boyfriends or exasperated, offended and irritated girls. Right or wrong, it is how he copes, he just needs to meet a female that copes in the same way and fancies him. There will be one, somewhere. So he's searching, the sad thing is that it sometimes takes a punch in the mouth for him to get the message to 'walk away very fast in short jerky movements'. An even sadder thing is that when he's 'normal' and not talking out of his underpants (an interesting concept when everybody else in the room is talking out of their backsides), he's a star. There was a female client with the same personality mixture (she's the one who coined the phrase 'turquoise toss'). Everything was either very white, super, or very black, shitty. Neither had an in-between calm, grey area. They hated each other with a vengeance, mostly to each other's faces. (She died in 1998, two years after I met her, aged thirty, once met never forgotten). Saying 'No' politely to him wears a little thin, when each rebuke is U-turned as if you're lying. In the end, being off hand and not interested bores him to death, and he disappears—most of the time. Sexually disinhibited is his label, not taking 'sod off' literally is the outcome. He sustained his injury when he was sixteen, and as a result has stuck in this mould. We all know how irritating sixteen year olds can be, if we're not sixteen.

Back to the knock at the window. He had escaped his helper who is with him all day every day. He's not allowed out on his own. He came in through the unlocked door, although I hadn't invited him in. Hadn't seen him in action full flow before. His body language and verbal were beginning to scare me. Trying to make light I asked where his helper was? Did anybody know he was here? He shrugged and sniggered like a naughty child, asking what was worrying me, he wasn't going to touch me! "I haven't touched you yet—have I, no . . . so calm down." He was rubbing his hands together like Uriah Heep in David Copperfield. I said, "Nothing is wrong." as his helper appeared at the window. I got reprimanded for letting him in? Can you Adam and Eve it? Maybe it's because of this, that to this day my front door is always locked, with the chain on (well you never know!). My helpers are really good. They do it now too (feeding my paranoia) when they close the front door. Even Teeny, my upstairs neighbour, does it. The amount of people that have asked with raised eyes, "You're locking me in?" to which comes my calculated reply, "So I can read to you . . . you can't escape!"

I did the signing class, still went to bingo sometimes, but didn't volunteer at the charity shop anymore. At the signing class was getting to know a very nice lady, married with two children. Xmas was near and cards had started going round. She made it clear, to save time and money, that Xmas cards wouldn't really be appreciated as she was a Jehovah's Witness, and they don't partake of Yuletide. Remembering as a student greeting a Witness at my front door, who reeled off quoted figures . . . I think he was new at this . . . as to the numbers of the chosen few. "What happens when all these spaces are taken? What if they are already?" I asked him. His eyes bulged and he waffled on a bit, but couldn't really answer. Maybe my classmate could! I asked her. She didn't answer either but suggested that they all come round to the bungalow to explain. The whole family came round to the bungalow to answer. Her husband didn't/couldn't clarify either and I'm still not sure that reading all those scriptures out loud provided any answers. I was surprised how totally wrapped the whole family was, about and for, this belief. I was impressed with such conviction and was intrigued now. Would anybody attempt to answer my original question? So I agreed to go to a meeting. I asked a lot of questions, 'why' being the first. I was led to believe that in Jehovah's heaven there are a limited number of places, and only if you're chosen and virtuous do you get a seat. What do you do if all the places are taken? Where do you go? More coffee and reading. The husband had given me a list of the relevant Bible passages which would enlighten me. He didn't answer either and kept reading passages from the Bible. Well . . . each to their own. No, it wasn't for me. I was miles behind, stuck on the no birthdays! and no Xmas! bit. Heathen that I am.

Unlike the Unit, the bungalow had a bath instead of showers. Hadn't taken a bath totally alone when I first moved in. Looking into the bathroom had caused massive fear waves. It had a tiled floor and there was absolutely nothing to grab hold of, to enter and exit the bath! "Why aren't there slip mats?" I queried, having visions of doing the splits or breaking something on this floor, after doing gymnastics to get out of the bath. I expressed my surprise; surely somebody else has been in here before me who, as a result of their head injury, was also dodgy on their feet? Felt a bit happier when the slip mats came. But bathing alone still raised scary monsters! This is where the bathroom routine started. It was such a painful experience and effort, when slipping and jarring yourself all the time, that when I got in—I did what I had to and—got out. To this day, I don't think I could lounge and loll in the bath. I also didn't wear any makeup. The few times it was tried, it took me longer to remove the mascara smudges than it did to put it on with one hand, the other anchoring me to the sink. Even so, concentrating on hitting my eyelashes meant forgetting that you're holding yourself upright and inevitably the downward jerk meant more smudges, all running, as the eye would be watering from the sudden poke with the mascara wand.

Doing ordinary everyday things like brushing your teeth were such a time consuming nightmare, dropping the brush umpteen times whilst slipping and trying to keep your eye on the end of your toothbrush. The eye that's still smarting from the mascara! Arty farty appearance stuff could wait, later. Although it seemed like a good idea, at the time.

When self catering in the Unit, the results of my labours were carried for me to the dining room. In the bungalow I had to carry it myself, and since I did eat, the kitchen floor was a pizza! Fortunately, the dining table was next to the kitchen door. I couldn't clean or sweep the floors myself, so everything and every room in the flat had to be vacuumed, regularly. But they weren't done that often, there wasn't a vacuum in the bungalow and I couldn't go and get the vacuum from the Unit on my own. It wasn't an upright vacuum that could be pushed, it was one of those that you have to carry the vacuum and great length of flex and the brush part, which I simply could not do with two sticks. Unless I carried it on my head!

I was still timetabled like everybody else, they had 'room clean' (one room)—and so had to hog the vacuum! I had four rooms, two of which needed to be de-pizza'd! I requested a trolley to carry food and drink about in the bungalow, and while they were at it, get one for the Unit! This would enhance independence when self catering. I explained that having a member of staff to always carry my gourmet delights to the dining room for me, defeated the object. With the trolley I could have done it myself, or at least tried! In the bungalow I would have coffee in the bedroom, in the bathroom, just because I could, with my new trolley!

When I was packing all my belongings to leave the bungalow I found some related literature with numbers and titles written all over it. Of passages that I was supposed to read from the bible. Enlightenment, they had given me one with which this would happen. Which was around somewhere.

I'm very special the cook made a cake for me when I left.

CHAPTER FOUR

My brother had a party at his new student digs and he invited me. I hadn't been invited to a party for years. Had a few drinks, as you do, so was very happy, as you are, and was chatting (flirting outrageously) with a really funny, good looking guy, most of the night. It's since been discovered that he was a gatecrasher and nobody knew who he was. I have no idea what happened to that man, or of his name, or what he looked like, but I know that he was pleasant of feature.

The toilet was upstairs and a hazard course, coming down after a visit was slow and clumsy. I was holding traffic up by blocking the stairway, having to hold the bannister with one hand and steadying myself on the wall with the other. As I was nearing the bottom I was aware that me getting down the stairs was grabbing attention, and saw two young girls covering their mouths whispering to each other whilst looking at me and sneering, "Look at the state . . ." I paused at the bottom looked at them and said, "I'm disabled." That shut them up and I carried on past them, they were apologising and I was sniggering under my breath, '. . . and drunk!'

I wrote this for my writing class. It's about my second and third Christmas's and I called it:

LUCKY BREAK

Well it hasn't been so lucky so far.
I don't know though . . . depends which way you look at it.

I hadn't seen Pathetic for months. So I paid to fly and see him, eager, as I had missed my last wedding anniversary. My mum had to go with me the first visit. Couldn't travel alone and she had to push the wheelchair and carry everything. So this was my first journey alone. 'Disabled' Change of flights too. I had to go back into the wheelchair at the airports. This upset me.

It had been my thirtieth birthday the day before. A big and clever birthday, in more than one respect. He hadn't seen me for months. I was disappointed. No flowers, no prezzies . . . just him. He bought me a walkman, for my birthday, I'd got one with me. He exchanged it for a watch. Very nice . . . I was wearing one I liked, that he'd bought me. Hot on imagination.

He carried on working, only Xmas Day off. For a month I sat in his flat, that I'd never seen before, watching the only English TV channel, which broadcast news ALL day, EVERY day! But, if World War Three had broken out I would have known about it! and promptly forgotten.

No, there were a few fun times—well it was Xmas! and although I cannot recall one time I'm just presuming there was one because it was Xmas. When I did go out I stayed seated, in the same spot all night, being talked over and around or patronised. My husband accused me of paranoia. I told him to just watch. Yes, it did happen.

New Year came. Party—midnight struck. One of the older guys I pecked, shoved his tongue into my mouth! Yuck! I was gobsmacked! He had a 'yes?' smirk all over his pathetic face. I told nobody, did nothing. Ass! I wouldn't have minded so much had he been nice.

We got back and really crashed out. I woke up, nature calls. Thirty seconds and counting . . . Crap on my feet anyway, I fell loudly and, bummer, bloody hurt myself! I heard him tut, say, "Fuck." then turn over. "Are you alright, Gill?" called half-heartedly from comfy bed at least, would have been nice. I was a bit hurt and annoyed, drunk! I crashed and wobbled, at the same time, back into the bedroom and did a fisherman's wife impression on him. He got up, ran, to my side of the bed, and punched me. On the arm, a kind of jabbing, 'so there!' punch. He was as surprised as me. I didn't hear what he said, I was gabbling away hysterically myself! It did hurt, he is a blackbelt. I thought that self control was part of martial arts—especially to that grade! He must have studied at the school of 'SMAKIN' WIFE'.

Horrendous nightmare!

Time to go home, back to the wheelchair again. Couldn't really have started any worse! I thought. I got in the wheelchair, I turned to look at my husband, and, he just walked off, and left me. I had to be pushed by airport staff. When I asked him, "WHY?" he said, "Because he didn't want me to see him cry." Well how about just being a little more thoughtful next time?

My flight itinerary was wrong, I was sitting next to some people that didn't speak English, they told me this. At one airport one of the staff was pushing me. "Could I go to the toilet, then a cup of tea?" I asked. "It's not my job." he answered. Not gobsmacked enough, "I'll piss in the chair, if you DON'T!" He took me. But not for the tea! Another disabled passenger, also wheelchair bound, and I, sat moaning and chain smoking, until our flight was due. I did write all this down for some (very, "Oh how awful.") air stewardesses. Nothing happened.

So, he hadn't seen me for another year. He called, November, "I'm not coming home for Xmas." he informed me. "Why?" I'd asked really confused. He couldn't afford it he clarified. "OK." I put the phone down. Hang on a minute, he's in the Middle East, rent paid, flight paid, petrol and fags virtually GIVEN away! His only real expenses were food and drink. Cheapskate! or had he become an obese alcoholic? Anyway, floored by the idea of spending Xmas alone, I made plans. I would COOK, from scratch, my first Xmas lunch . . . EVER, for my family. If you're going to do it—do it good!

Why hadn't he invited me over? I asked him, well demanded of him, the next time he called me.

"Oh . . . I never thought of that . . . come over!" With that persuasive invitation, along with thoughts of last Xmas. "Erm . . . No, I've made plans." I replied.

He didn't call me on Xmas Day. He didn't call me on New Year's Day. I called him, he 'couldn't speak to me, he was at work, he'd call me later'. He didn't. I called him again, this is not nice, what's going on? Why are you being such a thoughtless bastard? "I'll call you later." He did, "Gillian . . . I don't know how to tell you this . . . I've got somebody else." He was crying, what for? Because he'd got somebody else? was she that bad? (Meow). I was squashed, again, emotionally this time. My brother, "What are you whining for? You didn't want him back anyway!" THAT'S NOT THE POINT! It wasn't. He hadn't seen me for a year, I'd got my own place, a lot had changed. Me.

"Marriage is for better or worse Gill! of course I still love you, when you come back . . ." I must admit that I did wonder how long this garden path was, and as we all know, actions speak louder . . . Wakey, wakey Gillian. OK . . . Gillian died. He didn't really give Mark Two a chance. BUT, I didn't know that Mr Black Belt was, basically a pathetic wuss. Lucky break?

CHAPTER FIVE

THE THIRD YEAR

A ground floor flat was found, near to my parents. I was taken along to view and approve, but needn't have bothered. I was going to say yes, whatever it was like. Well, a converted Victorian vicarage, with an old church in my front garden. Yes. Yes, yes!! A new conversion, but there had been one tenant in my flat before me, who, on leaving, took everything with him, including the lightbulbs. If he had them. But, he did leave a pile of dirty rubbish in one room, how kind. No furniture, no carpets . . . nothing. Yes; even though I owned absolutely nothing that was even vaguely practical and useful for setting up your home. Loads of pretty junk, though. So I moved into an empty shell that was painted a totally bland magnolia throughout. Signed the tenancy agreement and I could move in, after a few essentials had been sorted. I was quite happy to move in with a bed, kettle and ashtray. Met my new support worker (Spruce Girl!), and it all started. The first thing donated in my needy direction was a dining table with four chairs from the Unit. I don't understand this. Expensive new tables and chairs were bought for the dining room in the Unit. It looked very nice What was wrong with the others? They weren't broken and they did the job, they didn't look that bad. The cash should have been spent on food, as it was cheap and nasty in my opinion. But I'm just a head banger, my thoughts and opinions are inappropriate. They were just going to dump the old stuff. I'm pleased, as one of the dumping grounds was my new front room. The Unit handy man (aka Turnip Slicer), came to help me get the place sorted before I moved in. Fitting the grabrail above the bath, which I didn't use for a week because it was full of pictures, but when I did, I found the grabrail to be essential. I'd bought four wooden trellises even though I couldn't use them, "You haven't got a garden." One was put on a wall in each room, a good idea. If it's important it's on one of the trellises, somewhere. A chain was put on my front door, I was quite insistent about this. Paranoid or what?—there was a buzz on my intercom, I didn't know this person. He explained he used to live here and that he hadn't got a key to get in! "That's maybe because you don't live here any more." I remarked. Told him that he hadn't got any mail, and that I was sure that he hadn't! I haven't spoken to him since.

Looking at my new window, there were painted screws in the surrounding wooden panels. "What was behind them." I wondered aloud. "Probably a dead cat!" the handyman suggested whilst taking the screws out. Original wooden shutters, folded away, was the answer. I still proudly display these to most new visitors.

The Salvation Army were approached by my new social worker. Could they help this needy person who had NO furniture—at all—and no money? I was decidedly needy. "Pathetic" was, of course, no help, in any way, although he knew my situation. Went to the local Salvation Army to have a look at the furniture they already had in store. When I enquired about a coffee table, as in, I needed one so could I secure this one? (it was the best of a bad bunch, and they were trying to sell some of this junk!). No, I wasn't allowed to choose, they would send what they thought I needed. He prodded at his clip board, "It sez 'ere that you need everythin'—'cept a table!" He nodded efficiently. I smiled, bless! The desperately needed furniture came—minus a coffee table. There was a large, old, ugly and terribly heavy wardrobe that was broken. My dad couldn't get the door back on. A sofa bed, which we HAD asked for, was dirty, ugly and smelly but better than nothing and intended for when my brother stayed over. It was uncomfortable to sit on as well as, apparently, to sleep on. (The case reviews are now held at my place. I recall the review when two people were sat on this sofa. The meeting concluded and everybody was leaving. Except these two who where still seated. Silence. One turned to the other, "Can you get up?" The other giggled, "No!" It was a very low, uncomfortable, eyesore. My student brother took it, and I think it's rotting in peace in a garden somewhere now. Making a comfy bed for slugs). I bought a replacement that's clean.

A dressing table with drawers and a set of drawers were next. I had a brilliant idea to tackle the lack of space. If we take the legs off both, they can be stacked one on top of the other. They won't look so bad, and they'll take less space I reasoned. My support worker, 'Mr Ego', scratched his chin agreeing. The cheap drawers were first: taking the legs off was easy, they screwed off. I couldn't do the dressing table. Mr Ego, who had been grinning and watching me dismantle my furniture, tried. It wasn't until the dressing table was completely destroyed that we realized that the legs were holding it together. Oops! We did rescue the mirror, which is now on a wall.

Seating—an old fashioned set of three high seated chairs. Which also smelt and were dirty. "They're better than nothing!" I was told. "No they are not." was my reply. They were put in my bedroom, and never used. I was sitting on my dining suite chairs (doesn't that sound posh), insisting that bare floors were nicer than those chairs! I have absolutely NO idea what happened to them. I know that the chairs WERE in my bedroom, I took a photo of them. Probably entertaining slugs too. Another sideboard, which was OK. Very large and I didn't really know where to put it. A space was found—temporarily, I hoped. An ottoman which I intended to paint from BLUE to a colour that was nice. When I bought the new paint I liked the colour, but it was a nasty orange when opened, still. Had great fun and fortunately there was still no carpet on the floors.

The bed, a requested double as 'I'm married!' came. A mattress, a base and a headboard, on a wheeled frame. The dressing table dismantling support worker (Mr Ego) and I, with clumsy difficulty, constructed the framework for the base and mattress. With even more difficulty we managed to lift the base above the frame. Nothing was said as we gawped in disbelief when the base crashed onto the floor missing the frame. It was a King-sized frame and a double-bed sized base. They'd sent the wrong pair! Kept the mattress and base, which are still on the floor, the headboard being stacked against the chairs. Spruce Girl said that I, "Ought to buy a new bed!" Why? I like it. "It looks stupid, and you're always stubbing your toes!" I like it and I'd stub my toes on whatever bed I had. It's not the bed, it's the way I walk. I was told at the Unit that I walked like 'Aunt Sally', a character from Worzel Gummidge, a TV programme. My mascara didn't look too dissimilar either.

So there I was, terribly disappointed about the furniture and still carpetless. There are still dirty handprints on my magnolia walls as a momento of this time. Superficial home improvements were happening. Pictures, shelves, toilet roll holder, coat hooks, trellises, towel rail, mirrors and then (roll of drums) CARPET! Wey hey! I was taking photographs, of the stages, as all this was happening. I'm chuffed that I did this, the before and after shots are so totally different. The AVS— another charitable organization—donated some furniture. Playing the same role as the Salvation Army. It doesn't exist any more I understand. I hadn't requested anything from them and hadn't parted with any money, as I'd had to for the Salvation Army delivery. Fifteen pounds delivery charge, and they are just around the corner. The AVS provided a TV table, which I needed, another sideboard, which is nice, a two seated chair, comfy, a high backed chair, clean, and another ottoman (not blue or orange). All of which are in use to this day. Both chairs were brown too AND went with my NEW brown carpet. Nicely!

And now for the 'piece de resistance' as far as furniture goes. My dad's neighbour showed me this huge wall unit that he was storing tools in, in his garage. "Could I use it?" he asked. At the time I wasn't that impressed, but answered, "Yes—I could use it, I think." It was in his garage as it simply, wouldn't fit in their house. He and his son dismantled it, transported it to my bedroom and reassembled it. As I have such high ceilings it fit—perfectly! wow! it's brilliant, now my favourite thing. I fell on my feet for once. I was getting a bit fed up of falling on my head.

(I haven't told you, this is my second pretty major head injury. The first: I was newly graduated and went to work in a bar with friends in Corfu. I was on the back of a motorbike with a newly-found friend, an English guy that had been there for thirteen years. The party ended when I woke up in hospital the next day. Basically, he'd crashed and I have no idea what happened (yet again). I ended up in the equivalent to the National Health Service and was quickly moved by my friends, to a private hospital, where I was in a ward with one other person. At one point there were two Gillians in the ward which led to a very confusing exchange of words with a Greek nurse, ending in me being given an injection. Didn't think about it till the other Gillian looking at her watch said, "They're late." Discovered the injection was for her lung disorder. Punched a Greek doctor, with reason, because he was leaning on one injury whilst tending to another and continued to do so, although I'd told him to stop. This meant that subsequent consultations involved him opening the room door, poking his head round and asking, "You OK?" and didn't wait for an answer. I was in this hospital for two weeks and then flown back with a nurse escort. But that's another book, now back to this one. This does remind me of a routine I have now. A girlfriend that I was working with at the time told me that she was an 'expert at putting on clothes that were inside out'. I think of her often at night when I go to bed and my pyjamas are inside out again. Alternating each night with the way I take them off. I always used to put them the right way, now I can't be bothered. If they are inside out tonight, they'll be OK tomorrow. Routine).

The Salvation Army was called and told that the furniture (aka rubbish) that they'd sent was no longer needed. Thank you. Could they pick it up and take it away? Please, so you can give it to somebody else. Could I keep it for a few weeks? they asked, then they might be able to pick it up. No,

I had no room and I didn't want it. My flat resembled the set of Steptoe and Son. It would be in the shed when they wanted it. They never came, obviously they didn't want it either.

Sitting in my elderly neighbour's front room, drinking tea and looking around as you do. She had lots of open space and little furniture. I envisaged the sideboard here. My mum and dad were due round for a visit. They ended up carrying the sideboard from the shed up some stairs into my neighbours front room. It was exactly the right size and shape for the room and space. I expressed my amazement, it looked brilliant. Phew! I was pleased, so was she.

The broken wardrobe was made homeless by the new wall unit taking up the space. Gutted! My dad made me a chunky metal clothes rail to replace the wardrobe. Each room was nearly sorted now. My cooker and washing machine are rented, to keep life simple.

Well the curtain saga has ended, and they look the same to me. I'll explain. A few months ago, I was closing my bedroom curtains. They closed, with a loud sickening crash, in a big heap on my bedroom floor, at my feet, with the curtain rail. Tut. 'It's too late to call my dad', I reasoned, so I telephoned him the next day. He'd 'try and get round later', was his response to my dilemma. "No," I said, "please get round later, I'm female, disabled and live alone in a ground floor flat. I'm bothered that my bedroom curtains are rugs in my bedroom." He came later and put them back up, and told me that, "It was a matter of time before it happened again." Brilliant (it's a Victorian house so the ceilings are very high—just to make life interesting and make it impossible for me to change lightbulbs!). Anyway, as a result of me 'yanking' at them and the rail being a cheap, dodgy fitting one in the first place, combined with my crap sense of balance (which is part of my disability), they hit the deck. Well it was, apparently, 'inevitable' and 'a matter of time'. He told me to get a curtain pole, with rings. So I did, the next day. He was sent a post card from York a few weeks later. "Hello daddy! Thought of you, you gonna put my curtain pole up or what? Love—Gillian. x." On the phone a few days later I asked him 'did he get the postcard?' He laughed, 'yes he'd come round and put my curtain pole up!' Nice one. As he'd have his tools anyway(!), in my nicest voice I asked, "Could you put a bathroom cabinet up too please?" Bathroom Cabinet? I didn't know I'd got one either! Explaining that I'd been to a local market auction and bid for a footstool—like I need more junk!—and ended up with a bathroom cabinet, a grubby laundry basket and a small cream, slightly battered suitcase full of books dated 1956-1971. All the same 'lot'! oops! You should have seen us getting it all home! I was loads of help, well at least I DID try. Support workers have their uses.

The bathroom cabinet was a bit broken but not unusable, and better than the one I hadn't got. Yes! He'd put that up too, 'since he'd have his tools'. I eventually located the curtain pole, which had been put out of the way, tidily—somewhere. He came and put up my cabinet but needed a strip of wood to do the curtains. Which I wasn't that bothered about any more. If they were on the floor I would have been, but they weren't. Interest was quickly lost. Bothering me was the fact that I could now see myself whilst brushing my teeth! Yes!

So the curtain pole was postponed again. Days later, he turned up with the wood and I left him to make the coffee for break time, in air that was turning blue and irritated. He was SURE that it was the right size. "Tut . . . Damn . . . Damn . . . tut . . . !" was the running commentary. He convinced himself that it COULDN'T be used, in any way, sat and had coffee. The curtain pole was postponed. We spoke a few days later, had he got the wood, I enquired. Oops! No, he'd forgotten. Could he come round and do some work on my computer? he asked. Of course, was the reply, whilst it's printing you can put my curtain pole up! We agreed a time. Which I forgot to write in my diary, and subsequently just forgot and went out. He had to hand-write his work and was understandably a bit miffed that he'd been sat outside for half an hour. He checks that I've written everything down now.

The curtains were postponed . . . My curtains were starting to become a real issue, for him too. Day and time having been checked and paranoidly re-checked, he came round and I was in. Good start. No! He STILL hadn't got the wood. He found pieces of wood around my flat that I had saved for something, but what. It obviously was a good idea at the time. I have no idea what they were for. If they are ever needed, I at least know where they are—holding the curtains up. Whoa . . . spoke too soon. The wood is holding the POLE up! We could not get the curtain ring attachments to fit onto the curtains, and hence make them hang from the pole. No way, no how. My dad had his determined head on; it was the way he jabbed his glasses up the bridge of his nose whilst muttering that he was going out, "To get something." He prodded a hole in the wood of every ring, and an 'eye' was screwed in. So each ring now sported a redundant lump of plastic and a screwed in eye. We still could not fit the rings onto the curtains. NO! Let's have another coffee, we can do this! Hey look! If you actually thread the eye THROUGH the curtain, it works! My curtains are hanging where they should be. The original fittings are still on each curtain. Plus each new ring has two fittings, and one of these is through my curtain. As there are ten rings on each curtain, you could swing on them now, and they wouldn't fall on your head. You can smash through the window! but the curtains will still be there! hanging, swinging . . . My mum looked at them, "You needed hooks." and added, "Your dad knows nothing about curtains. I used to do them." Now she tells me! They look the same to me, not that one sits and stares at curtain fittings you understand. They open, they close. They work. So the curtain saga is over. For now. They'll need cleaning at some point. Can you clean curtains whilst they are still hanging?

One Wednesday morning about eight o'clock, I was awoken by vacuuming upstairs. A bit disgruntled but it was the first time (explaining my bad mood away). The following Sunday morning, at eight o'clock, the same alarm call. NO!! Wobbled upstairs knocked, loudly, on their door. NO, it's SUNDAY!! They had been doing the same thing for a year, why hadn't I been bothered and said anything before? I don't know. But it's bothering me now. Fair play, this encounter was a one off because they moved out.

I was given a bird, it wasn't a budgie, a parakeet or a canary. Of course he wasn't! I could spell these. When writing to friends telling them of the new—messy but gorgeous—feathered lodger—he was a cockateel, a cockateel . . . got it now. Cockatiel. The 'spellcheck' facility on my new toy is a bit good. I don't know if the 'old fashioned, takes a bit of effort', method of looking it up in a dictionary would ever have happened. Sign of the times? or sign of laziness? When he was delivered by my mum I could not believe how happy I was. A bloody bird! Who came in a small dirty old cage, with his water bowl in the bottom. No matter where this was moved, he always managed to crap in it. So, when alone he obviously goes into combat mode. Lobbing sunflower seeds everywhere and bombarding his water bowl. Should my reaction therefore be, 'Yeah!! Good one! Who IS a clever boy!'?, or 'Bloody hell, TART!'? when he's made such a mess. Changing his water meant carrying the full vessel of soiled water to the kitchen, it never needed emptying when I got there, because I'd got soggy, seedy green trails marking the route from him to the sink.

I won at bingo!! So he got a new big posh home, with the water dish fixed on the side of the cage. His new home arrived. The person that brought the cage round offered to transfer him. Did I have any gloves? he asked. Gloves? "He's got a BIG sharp beak." I didn't have gloves that would fit him. I offered a dry dish cloth or a tea towel. Well, he made a clumsy grab for the bird, who had a complete fit. Noise? Big flight feathers everywhere. I had a complete fit. This guy, trying to help, had the bird and me freaking in stereo. The man had the bird clasped in his hands, turning to calm me down. I was getting screechy, noise—loud, me and the bird, and feathers—loads. I looked down at the bird. He was squinting with the effort of holding onto a big chunk of finger. I was horrified. I'd had him one week. I'd bought him a clean posh new home with unpolluted water and now he'd got absolutely no tail! It was all in the bottom of his old cage, and he wasn't! I was trying to calm the still distressed bird down; I too was irritated. "Excuse me." I turned, he was standing with his throbbing finger held out, "Do you have a plaster?" One-all?

Got him a new mirror, cuttlefish, honey bar and millet. The cage came with a bell! It's a good job he's got a big cage, he still fits in—just. Once settled into the new cage, he decided to explore the wider surroundings of the flat. I was very encouraging, "Come and look at your new digs." He came out. Flew round the room once, wonkily, and crashed full throttle straight into the window. Thudding to the floor with a loud distressed squawk, shedding a few of the feathers he'd got left. He wobbled under my table, and left a heap of gratitude. I carried his cage over, the handle broke and the whole thing self-destructed. He 'thanked' me again and left it under the table.

His tail-flight feathers!—have grown back now, but he doesn't come out. Either he's forgotten how to fly or he's got so much food, distractions, that he's like, "No . . . I like it right here—thank you." My mum says he's getting fat, but he's still gorgeous and I haven't noticed! I was impressed, no amazed, he still managed to crap in his water! And the container's fixed to the side of his cage? I got a special bird water feeder, ha!! He puts seed in this!

When he came he was called 'Joey', Yuck! I renamed him Bird. I was rabbiting away to Bird and he was quiet. 'Who IS she talking to?' I got bored and wandered off. He started talking! I wobbled back, he shut up! I, disgruntled, left. You've guessed! He started, "Joey's a pretty boy!" He squawks, and yes it's OK—for the first ten minutes. "SHUT UP!" will be the first thing he says, most probably when he's got a large audience who will think I taught him to say that. Actually! . . . I find seed in the most outrageously strange places; oh yeah and bird doings! When I go out he must get armed up with missiles—sunflower seeds. "I know I'll see if I can hit the TV with this . . . wang . . . yeah! now the hi fi . . .

yeah!...chair...nope...hi fi...yeah!" He's got a brain the size of pea, he surely can't remember the tail incident. I'm quite happy to sit being a novelist, coffee and fags! He seems quite happy to stay in his cage eating honey bars and millet, feeding his water container with seed! But, he is gorgeous, and funny. He's been a resident here for months now. I left the cage door open—for weeks. I kept forgetting to close it when I went out, but he didn't venture forth—he couldn't take his millet with him.

He comes out now. Not very much and not very far, he's still a bit rubbish at the flying stuff. He was in my bedroom and I wanted to go to bed. He still won't let me touch him and after a while of chasing him around and him avoiding me, I was irritated enough to go and get his cage. Bringing the mountain to Mohammed...which meant of course seed and water from the front room to the bedroom and on my bed, on which I had to stand to get the cage door to his height. Trying not to empty what was left of his seedy water onto the bed, standing on a mattress is hard, got the door to him and smacked him with the cage. He let me do this twice—bloody bird! (As I write the end of this book, a year on, this is sorted, he's a love!, I uncover him in the morning and open his cage door. He now flies about freely, visiting his home to eat and play noisily with his bell (usually when I'm on the phone)! I cover him up when I retire. He is as free as he can be, landing on my head now when I'm on the computer, pushing my hair into my eyes and onto my face whilst pecking furiously at my hairslide. Teeny pushes him off her head, "He's messing up my hair!" I look like a bad hair year).

Going to my postbox one morning, I noticed that there were three Xmas cards displayed under my 'tree' creation, which I'd made for the communal hallway. Ah how nice, entering into the spirit, then wondered who they were to and from. Had a look, 'To Gillian', picked up the next one, 'To Gillian'. They were all mine and somebody had opened them for me, I was understandably a bit cross. A young man had moved in upstairs. Mail was opened and cheques were stolen. Didn't have chance to get to know him, he disappeared as quickly and quietly as he came.

Think I spoke to him once. Another new guy replaced him in the flat upstairs, he asked if he could have the furniture left in the shed. By all means! So it's all found a new home. I still don't know what happened to that 'super' chair set nor if the new neighbour has managed to fix the wardrobe. The elderly neighbour died, and so the new neighbour also ended up with the sideboard. It's already been in three flats out of six in this building alone.

Once I moved into the flat, I knew that I would still be having reviews with my social worker and everybody else who is involved with my case (I may be accused of being shirty here, well I don't care). I knew where my review was—at my place—and what date (that was the message and information given to me by Spruce Girl). No, I insisted, if I don't get a letter stating this, the review isn't here. This is my home, you can't all just invite yourselves round, meeting or not. "But I told you!" reasoned Spruce Girl—my point exactly. "What about civility and manners? I only have a head injury." repeating, "This is my home." I got a letter and the review went ahead. If there were any negative ripples I smoothed them with filter coffee and cakes. Respect isn't a big word but it means a lot.

Well, I don't know . . . earlier I went to see some friends. So there were two other clients, me and my support worker sat drinking coffee. I told this joke:

What do you call a rabbit with a bent cock?

. . . Fucks Bunny . . .

The two clients guffawed. My support worker, quiet for once, had a 'What?' look on her face. Bloody hell . . . she didn't get it. Oh my . . . I tutted loudly, FUCKS . . . FUNNY!! She laughed. I've JUST pieced this together. I think this is funnier than the joke. As everybody else, including me, was sniggering, she was smiling, but had a furrowed brow and the smile was a bit set, plastic. Talk about confused.

I told my case manager that I wanted to go to the Harrogate Flower Show, it looked interesting. Support was needed as far as getting there and I couldn't, and didn't want to, go alone. So off, Mr Effishent (one more support worker), and I trucked. "My wife would love this!" he kept saying all day. So would I if he'd kept quiet! I bought some fudge, and now know that flower shows aren't really for me—yet; well I haven't got a garden for a start. A pretty mediocre day obviously as this is all that I recall.

I had to go along to my local health surgery to register. Spruce Girl went with me. We went in to see a female doctor and sat down. She asked a few basic questions, writing down the replies. Then she asked where did my parents live, did I have any brothers or sisters, did he live at home, why? I stopped answering then and asked what this had to do with my medical records? Which were all with my previous Doctor anyway! and laughed, "and I've got cream knickers on!" She didn't laugh but said: "You're being a bit aggressive!" in an authoritative voice. "One of us has lost our sense of humour!" I said as I was getting up to leave.

At one stage I never seemed to be away from the surgery and have seen nearly all the doctors—except the one I'm registered with. There are two really OK Doctors at this surgery. I visited one (the one who I see the most) with a list, so I didn't forget everything. I could feel some lumpy bumps on my crown. My brother had looked for me, telling me that dad suffered psoriasis on his scalp so go to the doctor. The doctor looked at my scalp whilst I was telling him about these freckled things that are appearing all over my body, believing that they signified 'something else'! He looked at them too and then sat down, arms resting relaxed on his chair: "You've got dandruff and you're getting old." Good. I haven't got dandruff anymore, but those darn freckled things they just keep on appearin'.

CHAPTER SIX

Another support worker—Stickler—another supermarket jaunt. This supermarket has all the fruits and vegetables brightly enticing you in the entrance. Duly seduced by some BIG, RED SHINY cherries, I picked one up, not knowing whether I liked them any more. I put it in my mouth . . . um . . . no. "I'm SO disappointed!" What? I turned round. Yep! she was talking to me. Why? I'd stolen a cherry that's why! Is that it? Really?—I composed and rationalised my actions, or thought I did. What would I do if caught on camera? and stopped at the checkout? Well, I'd pay for the cherry, no I'd pay for two, and then get a free coconut! I quipped. Well I thought it was funny.

Teef Geezer, Stickler and I were wandering round Leeds town centre. My feet were causing so much hassle that I had to link arms with Stickler. Hobbling through an arcade a big fat woman barged into me so hard as she was passing, that if I hadn't been linking she would have knocked me over. Rather vexed I 'swung' round to look at her, "Stupid cow!" The man she was with said something to her, she didn't say anything. I got severely spoken to by Stickler, who was 'disappointed' again. She had to write in her report that I'd reacted 'inappropriately'. Teef Geezer was confused by her reaction so he asked his mates what they would have done. By all accounts I was 'too nice'—I should have smacked the fat bag with my stick—which she had knocked flying.

I have gradually weaned myself off using any walking aids, by choice, as my confidence and sense of balance have improved. My gait is still obviously wrong and as a result I still get gawped at. I'm still pretty hopeless in crowds and with not having a stick it isn't apparent—until I move—that I'm unsteady on my feet. I was at an ice cream van just the other day. The ground outside the hatch was rough and uneven and I overbalanced and stumbled whilst giving my order. The guy serving looked at me knowingly, nodded and smiled, "You 'ad a few, or what?" He was still smiling. "I wish." I replied. He stopped smiling and looked confused. Bless.

So, after a while of being buffeted, bumped and jarred in crowds when I'm sore physically and mentally, I concede and go home. I can't mutually side-step when walking towards people, as you do, I can just 'walk'. As a result I get snarls and gawps of disbelief when people think I'm being ignorant, more so if they've got a stick. I get almost wholly audible snipes from ignorant, rude and dense people. On the other hand, and just as annoying, I get the 'Ah' of understanding from stupid little people who simply cannot or do not deliver. The all-gob, no-action brigade, there are millions of them—you must know some. Why don't they just SHUT UP!

In the railway station after a journey to Leeds I was coming down the stairs—with no stick and holding the banister. (It's still horrendous coming down steps or downward slopes as I proved yet again when Gadget Boy and I went to Italy in Year four). An elderly gentleman drew up beside me with a stick. Coming equal to me, he put his head down in concentration, jabbing the steps with determination. A race was on. Competitive head on, I joined in. He almost threw himself off the last step, but he won.

Out with Spruce Girl in a local bric a brac shop (another one), at the top of some stairs, just looking at which side there was a banister, when another elderly guy, with a stick, came to the top of the stairs almost colliding with me. Whilst I was deciding where to transfer myself, he was holding the banister and filling the rest of the stairway with his stick. I didn't know what to do. Looking at him, he had a sneering look of complete disgust on his ugly mug, which he then transferred to Spruce Girl!—she was in the firing line again. I was supposed to move out of his way, he'd got a stick and fought in the war! I was bothered about this, as not being able to move fast enough, I didn't deserve such a disapproving look. Chuntering to Spruce Girl about this—he should have shown some respect for me—then it would have been returned—but I didn't fight in the war and didn't have a stick or an orange badged forehead! The world doesn't owe him a living! All that and I don't even know if he fought in the war! Whatever, his attitude stank.

Feeling confident but scared I decided to go out, alone, without my stick. Locked my front door thinking, 'there!' and out into the wide world I went. I obviously got stared at but didn't really notice as I was staring at the pavement (for uneven surfaces). I could hear them though, complete strangers. I passed two young men and overheard one of them say (I do hope that I wasn't meant to), "Look at state of 'er! She's so pissed!" To which I overheard the reply, "Na, she's a spacker!" Bloody no, my first time without my stick and that's what I look like! Told my mum who said, "You should have bashed them with your stick!" It was said, I hope, because I didn't have it! I enlightened her. My confidence was smashed and I went back to the stick, which I still felt I walked worse with as I tended to rely on it too much. I'd end up carrying it with the handle looped over one shoulder. It was still getting in the way and I was still very clumsy with it, but used it on steps or very uneven ground and you could see I wasn't 'pissed'—even if it was over my shoulder a lot of the time. If I hear them again, the two rude men, I owe them.

I was linking arms with my mum and walking towards us was a woman who was looking AT ME with complete loathing. She passed, I turned to ask my mum, "Did you see that?" My mum had turned to me with a look of complete confusion and disbelief. Yes, she'd seen it! Can you believe? The woman was about five foot four tall, and her legs were almost as wide and they were purple, referred to colloquially as 'Lardy Legs'. My mum is the only person that knows what I am talking about!

People around me have almost tried to force ROUTINE down my throat. Routines and behaviours that are normal and acceptable to them—the way they are. I don't really want to be like anybody else. Well I'm not like most now, anyway—and I probably wasn't before the accident, but it's about the only thing that hasn't changed!

"Write down in your diary when you change your bed!" I don't change my bed, nor do I write it down in my diary. Even if I did write it down, I'd probably forget to look back in the diary or that I'd written anything at all. Each night chastising myself, 'I must do my bed tomorrow', then get comfy and warm. When the sheets niffed, or were a bit crispy, I'd change them. I'm sure of that. I do love clean sheets, when you've just got out of the bath. I remember saying this to my mum on bed change day, "When I grow up, I'm going to change my sheets every day!" "Yeah, bet you will." was my mum's reply. Little did we know there'd be one day, so soon, when I couldn't even get in and out of bed—at all and then on my own. She was right, I don't change my sheets every day. "EVERY single time you go for a wee you MUST wash your hands." That was one of my favourites, and I should and I will.

I have discovered that I am not very good at ironing, standing still and performing with a hot iron is too difficult, I have the burn scars as a reminder. So Spruce Girl does it for me; I'm doing her a favour as she 'loves ironing' and who am I to argue? The first time she ironed for me she 'had to do my sheets and tea towels'! "No you don't." I told her, explaining that I didn't do this before the accident and wasn't that bothered now. They had to be done, she said as, "they look nice!" Towels and sheets get crumpled anyway on the first use, and I DIDN'T WANT THEM DOING! I carried on with what I was doing and turned to talk to her after a while. She was ironing a pillow case! I couldn't believe it and blurted the obvious, "You're ironing my sheets!" She laughed, "I've ironed two already . . . and a tea towel!" Rebel! I have to remove them from the laundry basket now otherwise she would iron them.

Routine!—I was going into a local bakery where they did addictive cakes, aptly called Yum Yums. They bake on the premises daily and the fumes waft through the door onto the street, having a 'Bisto Kids' effect on passers by. There is always a queue of drooling people, usually buying the same things that they always do. I always bought these cakes, at first it was two then three, then four, then they had a promotion for all us addicts. If you bought a pack of ten, three of them were free— effectively. The offer was snatched up, as I thought 'I'll be sorted for three days and one day will be courtesy of the bakers'. Well, it would have been had I not eaten them ALL that night. Not all at once! At the bakers the next day I was telling one of the girls that I'd done this and said that if I EVER asked for more than three again—she'd to say, "No, you fat cow." She reminded me of this later when I ordered four, having convinced myself that three was an odd number and that four wasn't really greedy—well not very. By buying them for my writing class, my reviews, my mum, my brother the method in my madness was that I could validly eat them too.

It wasn't broken but they fixed it—a loose analogy—they changed suppliers and the Yum Yums are horrid now. No matter, the cheese straws are the new thing and I get four of these each visit.

I have rebelled giving reasons against some of the 'routines' that are supposed to be part of my rebirth. I have, unwittingly, devised my own schedules. Each time I do the washing up, usually when I have to ie: no coffee cups or teaspoons, one gets carried away. If you're going to do it . . . or, don't do it at all. All or nothing—black and white. But, when this task is undertaken, the taps, washing up liquid bottle, plug hole and draining rack, all get a seeing to. Sinks have no excuse to be dirty—I'm OTT about my bath and toilet. The day that I have a dirty washing up liquid bottle and skids in my toilet is the day I lost it.

I scrub my coffee cups and teaspoons, a matter of having to since they will have been around for days, and end up scrubbing everything. I have enough scourers to see Xmas out, next year too, under my sink. I kept forgetting I'd bought some.

Teeny, making the ritual filter coffee, commented one day, "Spruce Girl did your washing up didn't she?" Showing me a badly coffee smudged mug. Two had to be washed again, I was a bit cross. Tackling this irritation with my usual decorum she was told, "What is normal for you in your home, doesn't apply here. My pots have to be scrubbed. It's that simple. You're not helping when I have to re wash them!" This reminded me of the time she had made me coffee and I moaned that it was too cold . . . "Does Bird make you coffee? No! . . ." she chipped. Good point.

The dustbuster, bought because of my messy bird, still dustbusts everything that it can until it dies. My spare toilet rolls are on display in my bathroom in a pyramid which is used and replenished. As a student if the pile of clothes by my bed weren't too crumpled or dirty they were worn again. Nothing's changed.

Going to the supermarket with Spruce Girl. I was getting slightly irate as I kick the trolley ALL the time! ALL the way round. The wheels get in the way of the way I walk nowadays. I'd got 'washing powder' on my shopping list; she picked up a bottle of fabric conditioner saying, "You need this." I didn't use it, I told her. She then went into sell mode on the virtues of fabric conditioner and why I should use it. I didn't use it, and I didn't want to, however 'marvellous' it was. I had to tell her to shut up, and kick start the trolley.

"You should have a bath and wash your hair every day." Spruce Girl advised in her supporting, good egg capacity. Bath times are a nightmare, I thought she knew that, and so I am quite happy to bathe every other day. "That's disgusting." I was told by somebody who has a bath 'every day' and washes her hair! She's got long hair too! If I did anything strenuous enough to smell and be dirty I'd have a bath daily, I argued weakly, feeling a bit of a tramp.

They were trying to suggest, strongly and more than once, that I do menu plans for each of the three meals a day I'm supposed to cook. I should cook from scratch; a happy, hunky dory, healthy meal, using meat and two veg. Yes, I should and would, if I was at all bothered and liked cooking. Add water, snip corners off packets, and bung it in the microwave that's the routine I like and should use. No, to making my life more difficult, I didn't like cooking before and I'll be damned if I'm going to learn that too. I DON'T LIKE COOKING! Cooking for a family is ENTIRELY different to cooking for one. My freezer is full of badly labelled left-overs from when I do have a creative spurt. There is a limit to how many times you can eat the same dish. Especially when you've made it yourself, and you're not a very good cook.

Another supermarket experience. My shopping list said, 'toilet roll'. "You need this." Turned to see what I needed, not again! It was a two roll packet of quilted, perfumed and scented bog roll for the same price (ish) as millions of rolls of supermarket own brand, perforated sand paper. Anyway, I don't want to encourage people to sit on my toilet for days admiring my toilet roll! "I use it!" she said as she put them back, and I picked up the boring stuff.

This poem was written for Gadget Boy after his first visit to my flat. He took me to the Lake District and we stayed at a hotel near Ullswater. We went walking; Britain has some incredibly beautiful spots—and we found one of them. A waterfall with a rainbow arcing into the plunge pool, magnificent! and I got a photograph that turned out but I've lost it. I was flushed with success as it had been a real walk and I'd got to the waterfall. Dinner that evening was earned and deserved.

HAIRY CHEST

It's back again.
How long?
Is a piece of string? Will it moult?
Will it fade?
Will it age and grey?
Hairy chests wander don't they?
Getting lost when they haven't got gadgets.

Mr Ego (yet another support worker—the dressing table destroyer!), really couldn't give a damn if you weren't being a pain and embarrassing. He took me and another client to a rock making factory by the seaside, that I really wanted to see (Willy Wonka's chocolate factory sprang to my mind). During this tour we went through the biscuit making section where they had trays full of broken biscuits for the visitors to eat. I had one or two and turned to talk to the other client—who could not answer and looked like a hamster. Swallowing, at last, he brushed crumbs off his face, "Got to get me moneys worth!" he smirked as he filled his mouth to maximum capacity again. We'd paid to get in, and from what I saw he was eating to get my money's worth too. We went along to the coast afterwards, looking for a fish and chips restaurant. Two of us were hungry. I noticed an orange disabled badge in a restaurant window, supposedly signifying 'welcome'. IF you're not disabled enough to use a wheelchair, you're quite welcome—if you can get in. There was a step leading to the entrance. I wouldn't have noticed this in my previous life. On this day at the seaside, I found a plastic bracelet with bits of glitter in. I wear it still.

Space Girl (my latest support worker), went with me to Leeds Art Gallery where they had an exhibit of art inspired by the human body. Nice theory but, yuck! Didn't inspire me to do anything but leave, to find something more agreeable. She also supports me in my taste; she didn't feel stimulated either. We liked many of the same displays, those with lots of detail—so she's evidently got disturbances too!

There is a local cafe that did nice lasagne (my favourite!) so Spruce Girl and I went often. The food was nice but the service was really dodgy. Two sisters own it—witch of the East and witch of the West—and one of them always seemed a bit odd and curt with us, on the verge of rude. We noted that she was very giggly with male customers. Even though I looked at the menu, I always had the same thing. It became a bit of a joke, so what ARE you going to have? but I liked it and knew I would enjoy it. Until . . . Spruce Girl and I were getting the contemptuous treatment again and I ordered lasagne. It came and the sheets of lasagne were raw, as in not cooked, the lasagne was crunchy and inedible. Having gestured the odd and curt woman over: "Is it frozen?" she snapped. "No . . ." reiterating, "It's not cooked . . . at all!" The plate was taken and she'd see what she could do. "No, that's OK, it's alright!" I laughed to Spruce Girl when the woman had gone. She returned, threw some money on the table, spat, "We haven't got any more!" and walked off. Nothing was said at first, we just sat staring at each other in disbelief. I could think of no reason why this woman was being so poisonous. Neither could my support who was always with me; I never went in alone. We narrowed it down to my disability, that was all it could be. I had to say something, that was outrageous, rubbish service too. On the way out we encountered the sister and tried to talk to her—and she was worse!

Another snide verbal assault and the first sister was round the corner by the microwave jabbing her finger in the air towards me and hissing, "I'm watching you! I'm watching you!" This is the point where Spruce Girl—my 'support' !—started to cry. I was completely mortified and didn't know what to do or say. Those two were still goading so we left; confused, upset and vowing never to return. I did go back with Teeny a few months later. She hadn't tried it and wanted to, but she knew of the incident there. That was months ago, I said, getting my things together to go out and eat. Must be in a time warp—they were still snarling. They are so disagreeable that Teeny, who noticed how bad they were, stated that she wouldn't return. She couldn't help but notice. We'd just been given our food and they started vacuuming. We couldn't hear each other very well, we were almost shouting at each other. "Excuse me." the vacuum was turned off and I'd got the floor space, "We're trying to eat and talk, do you mind? . . . are you hinting that we should be leaving?" Leaning on the 'broom' she replied "I didn't say that did I?"

Again, I could only conclude that it was something about me?

I've just found an envelope full of hair and plastic and it's reminded me to tell you about the time that I told my case manager (who was working with me at the time), that I wanted to do a parachute jump for Headway—another charity for something else (do we have a charity for being ugly yet?). She knew that the Parachuting Association won't entertain people that suffer epilepsy. Since I had described to her my experiences of, "Just—not being there for a second or so it seems, and not being able to focus mentally or physically—my sight always drifts to the right." she thought that these episodes were "absences—petit mals—a mild form of epilepsy" (Oh oh.) She went on to explain that after such a serious head injury that it was more than likely, most clients do. I was gutted—monsoons again—but it made sense, your brain is bound to be a bit upset and confused. What do we do with all this electric stuff? I know let's throw a party! we deserve it, this being awake lark is hard work.

She made an appointment for me to be involved with a neuro-surgeon, so I could be tested for epilepsy. This is called an EEG whereby thirty two wires are stuck onto your scalp to measure electricity produced by your brain, using gel that dries quickly so that the wires don't move (wish I'd taken my camera, I looked brilliant when the nurse had finished—my head was haloed in an Afro of multi-coloured wire). Then you have to lie down, get warm and comfortable—I liked this bit, then blink. Relax and stop clenching your jaw, I was told, and blink some more. Relax I was told again. I couldn't relax any more, my chin was already on my chest! After blinking for a long time the test was over. The nurse dabbed at my head with medical nail varnish remover so that the wires could be removed. It said on the appointment form, that shampoo was available on request. The nurse didn't mention it, I forgot and she'd dabbed at my head so I thought it would be OK. By now impatient to go. I'm not that keen to stay in hospitals when the appointment is over and I don't have to be there, even though I know most of the staff now!

Stickler said, "You look like you've got serious dandruff!" It only bothered me when bits of pink plastic were having to be fished out of my coffee, after I pushed my hair out of my face. Otherwise I couldn't see it, so I was bothered not, and I'd wash my hair later. Which I did. The next day I could feel plastic lumps all over my head, about thirty two, and I'd still got avalanche dandruff. My mum came round later and I showed her, saying that I didn't know what to do! I'd washed my hair twice and combing my hair hurt as these chunks of plastic were glued to the roots! She had to dab my whole head with acetone for about an hour. Annoyed, as I should have washed my hair at the hospital, but I didn't. Disturbed enough to have an envelope covered with written dates and times, full of hair and plastic. It'll probably be floating around for years—well I didn't get the 'Medusa' photo.

In the post a few weeks later I got another appointment for an EEG. Why? I've just had one—showing my Doctor the envelope of evidence. The first didn't show what they were looking for because I wasn't relaxed enough. Still slightly wary I sarcastically commented, "What, I'm not dead?" I had to take some sedatives before the next one, so I forgot to take my camera to take a picture of what I looked like. Relaxed and blinked and it was over. Insisted that my hair was washed, getting the envelope out again, and insinuating that I was going nowhere until this happened.

A blood donor session was being run locally, I'd had a postal invite as I'd shown willingness, having been a donor before. Off I tottered to do my bit. Got down the road and the building wasn't where I thought it was, and I didn't know where it was. Asked somebody that was passing if she knew. She nodded, and pointed across the car park. Got in, collected my number and sat waiting. After looking around for about half an hour my number was called. Answering the pre-donor questions, No, I hadn't been bitten by any stray dogs recently or injected myself with any dodgy hypodermic needles and I didn't know whether or not I suffered epilepsy. The whole procedure was abruptly interrupted, as I explained why, and I was asked to take a seat. My seat was still empty. The nurse in charge came to speak to me and took me aside. She explained that the change in your blood pressure, caused by giving blood, could induce a fit—whatever form of epilepsy you had. I cried. I couldn't even give blood and do my little bit. She asked if I was OK, did I want a drink? a seat? Thanks, but no—I have to go and I'm OK (I lied). By the time I got home I was—just one more thing.

A follow up appointment with the kidney guy, no problems there. Whilst we were in the same hospital we called in to see the neuro-surgeon (who was 'not afraid' of me as he told me the second time I saw him), to find out why I'd not received an appointment as a follow-up to the EEG. It had been months since the test, did I suffer from epilepsy or not? The answer was quite important to me! We sat and waited—well I looked around and saw leaflets on migraine and epilepsy. None, I was surprised, on Headway, which is a group concerned with head injuries—the consequences for you and your family during and after the brain trauma. I had not heard of them until year three of my injury. Have you? Well you probably will do sometime soon, as head injuries are becoming a normality—you will know somebody who has one or become one of the statistics yourself. This means another charity shop. They will all have to start selling stock to each other for a change of scenery—you can only hoard a certain amount of junk for a certain amount of time.

The neuro-surgeon saw us, I'd not received my appointment because they thought I'd moved. The first result 'couldn't be read' because I'd not blinked enough, as I was concentrating on relaxing my jaw. I did ask what they were looking for? The specialist peered at me, "Abnormalities." Well, that told me but didn't really answer the question and I didn't really know who he was, I didn't recognise him—at all. (The second test showed that I'm epileptic).

When I was about eight, I went away for a week with the school, to Hornsea (you'll see the reason for me telling you this shortly). I was only upset when I got a letter from home (the letter was kept for years, I've probably still got it!). All the kids were waiting for their parents outside the school gates, my dad's car pulled up across the road!—no, it's not them. They pipped the horn, and the headmistress asked, "Is that anybody's parents?" No . . . My mum got out of the car, "Gillian!" I still looked into the car before getting in, my dad had grown a beard. There you go, the doctor had shaved off his beard since I last saw him—just to remind me of this incident!. It also reminded me that the only time I was slapped on the leg by a teacher was at this school—for talking and sharpening my pencil whilst he was taking the register. I even remember his name.

My big toe-nails are slightly in-growing, a problem that is exaggerated because of the way I walk. I have walked around places carrying my shoes, as they were causing so much pain that I couldn't walk with them. I went to the National Health Service chiropodist—sorted for a while. My toe-nails grew faster than the next appointment so I had to try and dig at them myself, making a real mess and making them worse. The next visit he told me I'd have to have my big toe-nails removed. Surely that's not the only answer I argued, got scared and went private. No, my toe-nails didn't have to be ripped off at all.

The remedy was to grow them and stick strips of metal onto my toe-nails, to pull the edges out of my toe. They started to look like claws but felt alright for a while. Then they started to hurt. For some reason they started to cause me grief again. Back to the National Health Service. Saw a female this time. I had jerked my foot back, an automatic reaction to pain, as she dug into my toe to excavate some of the toe-nail. She grabbed my foot back tutting. "That hurt!" I informed her, thinking that I should explain. "Of course it did!" was her understanding response. It hurt so much that I couldn't put my boots back on. "Sit for a minute." she said, "Absolutely not." I said. She was informing me to make another appointment—I think she was saying under her breath, "Not with me." but I didn't hear as under my breath I was hissing, "Not with you!" I was in a dreadful state, I was so upset and angry and I couldn't walk very well at all. Spruce Girl couldn't say anything useful (no real surprise there).

In my art class I was explaining to a friend that I had a dental appointment that afternoon adding that I was looking forward to it! my dentist is REALLY good looking. "Mr Dentist!?" she exclaimed. She had the same dentist, and liked looking up his nose too. I was seeing him so often recently, that on leaving I was saying, "See you in . . . a few days!" rather than six months. He's heard all the parrot jokes to date, I see him that often. The original fascination he held, has worn off. I watch all that he's doing in the glasses he wears to protect his eyes. It must be really freaky having someone staring at you, but not looking at you, for as long as is necessary. Maybe that's why he chipped one of my teeth—that he doesn't know about yet.

CHAPTER SEVEN

I was living alone in the flat now with loads of time to kill and was encouraged to pursue any interests that I had, and I had none. There was little that I could do, and do alone, and I didn't know anybody. I was enrolled on a local college course by my case manager, one that I could do, that got me out doing something and meeting people, who happened to be like myself as in 'wandering', needing meaningful direction, and killing time. Which is what this course offered, one of those new fangled assertive courses. Usually run by unqualified 'teachers'. Teachers are unemployed, or blamed for kids killing each other (or it's the nurses or Israel).

Transport was ordered, reliable driving volunteers for the disabled—they charged five pounds petrol money. The people I met on this course were lovely, the students. The staff were dodgy and I found them a bit patronising. Some of the people I met on this course remain in my life as part of the 'Lunch Club' (the 'Lunch Club' was a group that was formed by a few of us that met at college and wished to stay in touch. It seems to have just faded, as good intentions do, which was inevitable I suppose, as none of us are in touch daily. A nice interlude though). We learnt how to say "No." decisively; if you do this already—or think you do—it's a bit tiresome. But it killed time, got me out and I met people. We did do some good stuff too—the buffet was nice.

My brother does Yoga and told me that I should try it, it was good for balance and the days that he didn't do it he "felt strange!" So I enrolled on a class for this too—more transport. The first time that I went I do recall getting this buzz. Obviously horrendous on the balancing parts and couldn't even try some, but was surprisingly supple for others, when you were sitting down. I also recall being very optimistic, in that I'll be doing handstands again soon!

After going a few weeks I started to leave incredibly frustrated with an awful headache. A headache where I don't feel that I'm functioning on all cylinders as it were. I still couldn't do the basic things—stand still and concentrate with your eyes closed (Don't we mean break dancing? I am a founder member of The Ministry of Funny Walks—Monty Python)! I started making excuses to myself not to go, then, well as you haven't been for so long, you just stop. Then, as you know that you should have gone and it would have been good for you, eventually, you're momentarily cross with yourself. Another vicious circle.

I've always been fascinated by cake decorating—sugar art—so enrolled for a class on this too. Again the people were lovely and weren't the problem, it was me. The cake couldn't be iced whilst sitting, so I had to stand up and ice it! Controlling standing up and icing a cake? I don't think so! I became a little disillusioned when every body else was icing dancing ballerinas and I was still trying to do straight lines. I kept going for as long as it took to produce an iced Xmas cake, which was actually very good, we had found a design decorated with white icing that was meant to be wobbly! Again, too frustrated, I stopped this too.

So I had a very busy week, yoga, cake decorating, signing classes and college. All needing the volunteered transport, which had been arranged. I was getting up and always ready when my lift arrived and all was going quite smoothly for a while. Uncanny. I'd been out with my mum and coming back, as I was late for the driver anyway, I was dropped off outside the local bingo hall where the evening session was just about to begin. I was seen by somebody who knew the driver, and they told him! He refused to give me a lift "ever again!" never spoke to me again either even though I tried to explain why I'd gone to the bingo. I didn't think he would still be there! and the session was just starting. I gave him a pile of jigsaws too! I had to get a taxi to college now! Bloody hell! It was four pounds. (As I'm typing this I'm getting incredibly cross with myself—what a failure! I write somewhere that, "I'm still searching for that thing." and I'll never find it whilst I'm still 'griping' about not being able to do things as I did. "Self denial!"—rings loud in my 'ears', mmm writing about it is one thing!)

I'd just got my new toy (word processor) and was dabbling with it. This creation is the result.

It's not always an enviable position, having lots of time to fill. Finding things that I could do, in my neighbourhood and alone. Well I'm still looking for that thing. So I started writing this on my newly acquired toy. This seems to be it, for the moment, 'the thing'. The book. As a result of this, I found out about and joined a local writing circle. Interesting.

A group writing competition was organised. The only guidelines were that your entry was, maximum, five hundred words long. Each passage was read out loud anonymously and everybody gave it a mark out of ten. The piece awarded the highest marks is the winner and gets a cheque and their picture in the local newspaper. This was my entry :

> What can you say in 500 words ?
> 6 down ! and counting . . . . .
> I'll tell you my newest joke.
> There's a parrot and this guy sitting on an aeroplane.
> Stewardess comes round.
> Parrot says,
> 'Get me a **** gin and tonic now! **** quickly! Slapper!'
> Man mumbles, 'Could I have a cup of coffee, please?'
> She comes back with the gin, no coffee.
> Parrot chirps, 'Get some **** peanuts to go with this **** gin! Slag!'
> Man mumbles, 'Erm a coffee please?'
> She comes back with the peanuts, but no coffee.
> 'Get me another **** gin! you still **** here?? Wench'

Man thinks, you have to be loud and obnoxious to get your order!
'And get me a **** coffee whilst you're there! **** bag!!'
She goes off. Bringing back with her a male steward, who throws them both off the plane. Hurtling, thirty thousand feet, the parrot turns to the guy,
"You're a bit gobby for some-one who can't fly aren't you?"

Now maybe you can help me here.

Do you think capital punishment should be re-introduced? The death penalty.

For the beyond doubt cases. The Myra Hindley's, Peter Sutcliffe's, Nielson's, Rosemary West's, of this world? Does it really matter why they did it? But prison should be available to punish those that have caused death by accident—they happen—for being stupid and thoughtless or a bit clumsy. With DNA testing and major forensic abilities you'd have to be in a plastic bubble to commit a murder.

Some of these people played God, in their sad minds, by abusing other people's God given right to life. Therefore don't they want to join Him and party? Peter Sutcliffe got stabbed in the eye with a pencil by a fellow martian, Hindley's got a degree. So what? They should be free? They've been punished and served their time? What? did I miss something here?

Are the victims alive again? These people haven't changed miraculously they've just been out of the way. A degree, a warm bed, three meals a day, no daily family nightmares, no heating bills and they have been proved guilty of MURDER, extinguishing a life. It is my opinion that if some were released they would re-offend, before they themselves were stabbed, they've got away with it once and will now appreciate how, if they weren't in prison would they have these things? Tax payers are financing this privilege.

Normal families not only struggled to put their own offspring through university but were supporting Hindley too! Disagreeable enough?

Totally unjustifiable when we are waiting for hospital beds, the National Health Service are suffering due to cutbacks. Education is suffering due to cutbacks. Single mothers are due to suffer, the disabled are next. Hit the weakest.

It costs approximately twenty five thousand pounds a year to keep a prisoner. It would cost us again if they were freed. Housing, jobs—allocated so they 'fit' back into society!—benefits if they're unemployable, protection. I think it's an unfair joke on the rest of us. Why should we pay for these people? "They have a right to life!" I was told unconvincingly. A right they forfeited by taking someone else's consciously. Top them! I say.

My case manager suggested that I do a newsletter for all the other headbangers—clients, and my mind was doing somersaults. I had a great time being editor and writer and I was happy with the result, I liked it. Stickler and I arranged to go to the rehabilitation unit by train, as I needed practice using public transport and I wanted to hear the client's reactions. Knowing already that there was one client who was offended by my use of the terminology 'headbanger', even though I referred to myself also. Find out if they had any thing else to say, any suggestions or ideas—I was playing the editor role with aplomb. We had phoned ahead to confirm visiting arrangements and to find out how to get there— using public transport. Off we went and changed trains as instructed. On disembarking we weren't sure of the way to the unit and so we asked, discovering that it was a very long walk, as we had been told the wrong station.

I have been asked many times, "How far can you walk?" My reply is always a considered, "I don't know!" We eventually arrived at the unit and I was in a dreadful mood and in considerable pain. How far can I walk? About that far.

When in the building I scanned the client's notice board, which was an indecipherable eyesore again, and as far as I could see my newsletter wasn't there. The clients that I spoke to hadn't responded as they hadn't seen it before now. But they liked and would reply to the copy I had with me. Discussing this disappointment with Stickler another member of staff suggested that the newsletter was read out to the clients at the weekly meeting, held each Monday (Moanday). Good idea! I agreed, and went off to find someone to put forward this proposal. I encountered the 'senior' occupational therapist, to whom I explained my disappointment. I had been asked to do this, I was told it was, "needed" and I was doing my bit! The clients needed prompting and reminding about most things and this is no different, and I asked why it wasn't on the notice board. I couldn't see it, I added, and I know what I'm looking for! In the first newsletter I'd made it very clear that if they didn't write then I wouldn't either. No, to writing a newsletter to myself. I therefore need replies! "If it had been interesting, they would have replied!" she answered. That shut me up. I left a little dismayed and joined Stickler, who was horrified when I told her. We left, after I had lashed the person that had given us the wrong directions. This is the first newsletter:

READ THIS . . . .

Where should I start? At the beginning? OK. I was born, a female (still am) 4lb 14oz, then . . . blah . . . blah   then I got a serious smack on the head. Putting it bluntly.
Hello, my name is Gillian, a fellow headbanger. One of you.
Why am I doing this? WHAT am I doing? Dunno . . . . . . got me . . .
I was asked to do a newsletter. So, here I am! It seemed such a good idea at the time.
God   I hate it when I do that.
So, you can help—I have no idea who I'm writing to, where you are, how many of you there are, what you want from/in a newsletter.
Or indeed, if you want one at all.
I'm happy(ish) to take on this commitment if it's worthwhile and appreciated.
You have to let me get to know you. So, if you wouldn't mind just answering these few simple questions :

Who are you?

Are you a youngish, male, unattached Woody Allen lookalike?

Well if you are—don't contact me, I'll contact you . . . . . soon . . . honest . . .

It was a JOKE!! I felt I ought to say that before all you 'Woodies' out there start sending me hate mail or something. Please do the something part—I cannot and don't really want to do this alone.

The ball is in your court—as it were . . .

Name, age, sex, locality, family, hobbies, general likes/dislikes, gripes, birthday. This info', from you!, would be a good start.

If you can think of anything else, anything—almost—get off your backside and fill me in.

This newsletter is supposed to be for you, by you.

Send your stuff to . . .

Relating to my case manager, who had 'started the ball rolling', what had happened at the unit. Agreeing that this response was totally out of order, not only as I had worked so hard, but also I was annoyed at the lack of professionalism. She said something to somebody, or told me she did. The newsletter just fizzled away and died. Staff in the 'Near Reach' sector didn't do their jobs either, and the clients just couldn't be bothered and forgot. It was just me again.

CHAPTER EIGHT

Spruce Girl and I bought a sandwich, she always has extra mayonnaise on hers. We were sitting in my front room eating, "This sandwich is orgasmic!" she told me. Looked across and she had mayonnaise smeared all over the bottom half of her face and smudging her lipstick! Never!? "Really?!" seemed an apt comment. Wish I'd taken a photograph now.

Started signing classes again, learnt how to sign my name again. Just to make my life simple discovered that some of the signs that I remembered where different for different regions. Excellent, who needs a simple life? The swearing signs were the same. I know the signs for car crash, four years ago and disabled. Sad isn't it. I know this as I said and signed this to the Tunisian entertainment guy, when he asked, "What's wrong with you?" When I told him his response was, "Bad."

With the signing class we went to the theatre where there is somebody stood in view interpreting. Well, I can hear and I hadn't got a clue what was going on. I'd get distracted by the signer, remember why I was there and concentrate. After a while of understanding one word in every sentence I'd give up and carry on watching the performance, and now I hadn't any idea who some of the characters where. When I'd clued in and knew what was going on I'd get distracted by a word, in sign, that I knew! Then I'd watch for a while, until I was lost again. I did this the whole play, so when I was asked if I had enjoyed it? I had to say, "I don't know!"

I must have 'one of those faces', as I was looking into a shop window and two rather snappy male Americans asked me if I could spare a few minutes? Could I? I could spare days. They were Mormons. They were very dedicated and came round for coffee, to guide me and answer my questions. Most of which were unanswerable as I'm a bit of a cynic, for lots of reasons. They came around quite a few times, I was getting to know them well. I went to one of their meetings, curiosity killed the cat. They eventually gave up and disappeared, my interrogations weren't answered though they tried. Again I was impressed with the almost tunnel vision conviction. Each to their own, everybody needs something I suppose. I've got another Bible. I think it's on the bookshelf, homing spiders and collecting dust with my teaching stuff.

Just closing the front door to meet Spruce Girl who greeted me, "Oh, you've got your brown jeans on too!" She'd got brown jeans on as well, how annoying. I ALWAYS wear brown jeans—they're my 'trade mark'! (with coffee spills and mug rings). A little disgruntled but nothing was said, they're only jeans and as she told me she'd got jeans "in every colour." Well I hadn't seen them, she usually wore blue I responded and ended the conversation.

Pathetic bought me a gold torque, a copy of a slave bracelet, for our first wedding anniversary. Mm. I wear it still, five years later. I was unnerved when Spruce Girl got a torque from her husband for Xmas, well he paid for it. She was showing me and being too glib. Remembering the jeans I was all of a sudden incredibly irate and brought this incident up and yes, there was absolutely no reason why she couldn't have these things! But the torque too! "Are you copying me?" I accused. "Why would I want to copy you?" was the cutting reply. I don't know—I just don't know!

My point was—this—me—is all that I have left. And it's mine. I'd like what are the good bits, to stay with me and not be emulated by the whole world! Flattering though it should be. She hasn't worn the brown jeans since and as my mum said, "She doesn't look as good in them anyway!" Ha.

I was out and about with Spruce Girl in my new neighbourhood. Getting to know a few people too, in the shops and my new neighbours— boosting my confidence to venture forth when alone. We got back and I walked into the kitchen, past the mirror in my hall. Backtracked and gawped in disbelief at my face. Mascara—making one eye almost black! "Look at my face!" looking at Spruce Girl, "Why didn't you tell me?" I demanded. "I didn't notice." she said unfazed. Tutted, "What? are you blind too? I'd have told you!" well, you should have seen me.

You should never assume anything, it makes an ASS out of U and ME. You have one mouth and two ears, use them in that proportion. These need to be spelt out for some people, unfortunately a number of these people are in charge of my life and judging me. I cannot cry, get all the appropriate despairing feelings but, the waterworks don't happen. My mum was distressed by this and the reason I was so distraught. "Here you can have some of mine!" she said dabbing at her eyes, "I can cry for England! I thought I was all cried out!" Pretty good life huh? somebody crying for me, driving for me, satisfying my husband.

If people say they are going to do things, why don't they do them? I go out of my way not to let people down, to fulfil my verbal commitments (if I remember them) or let people know if I can't. Not everybody is like me, shame. It particularly grieves me when I'm let down by the people who are paid to work with, and for, people with a 'head' injury. These are the people who tell me to write EVERYTHING down, so that I remember appointments and what I had for lunch two days ago. These are the people who shake their heads, tutting and sucking in breath, when I haven't.

I do, however, write down meetings and important dates. So aptly that my huge page-a-day diary is my guidebook, bible. I'm good with this now, if it's in front of me, writing down times and dates exactly and reiterating, underlining, starring and going over and around, so I can see it! Whatever reasons they gave: that 'I forgot' or 'wrote it down wrong', I knew what I knew, and stuck to my guns that I'd been sitting around for hours and maybe I did have something better to do. A phone call was

ALL that was needed, sealing my argument with the remark that, 'it was thoughtless and bad mannered not to and they'd have been annoyed had it been vice versa'. Point to me I think, they all ring and write to me about everything now. So I have to find a new gripe.

Being all determined and independent I'd ventured the train alone to see my brother, thankfully the large cumbersome candelabra that I'd bought at a carboot sale as a gift for him—was made of metal. I do wish I wouldn't do things like this! I'd told him what time I was arriving and said not to worry about being exactly on time, that I'd be waiting in the station bar.

Got off the train (well, fell off), my legs had gone dead with sitting for so long. So I walked even clumsier with the bloody candelabra down the platform to the bar, and the door was locked. Walked to the station's exit—no brother! Asked at the ticket office why the doors on the platform were locked. They didn't know. Went back to the front and eventually noticed that the bar had an entrance on the front. Sitting with my coffee, the bar starting to get really busy, as it was a Saturday night, I needed to rid myself of the coffee that had been drunk. This meant walking across the pub through all the people, who barged me, then gawped, muttered and sniggered. The stick made no difference—it couldn't be seen.

The return trip was the same and I shrugged it off. Sat back down having ordered more coffee, thinking that my brother would be here soon. When I had to go to the toilet the second time there was the same barging and muttering, but no sniggers this time. The snarls could almost be heard too. Sat down wondering what to do, I didn't want anything else to drink which would mean going to the toilet again, deciding that he must have forgotten about meeting me. He walked in and straight past me. Retracing his steps he laughed, "I almost missed you!" I didn't laugh, not even a little bit!

He said he liked the gift and carried it from here. He was explaining that he'd had problems and hadn't rushed as he knew where I was and that I was OK. He was right and I didn't argue much, well he did know where I was supposed to be, although I was upset. Well, I'm his only sister and he was there for me when this first happened, for which I am as eternally grateful as I can be. He 'forgot' my birthday. Can you believe it?

I rang his home on my birthday, having saved a posted Xmas card from him thinking it was a birthday card, and he wasn't there His girlfriend's brother answered and passed this on, "The message is, 'It's his sister . . . and it's my birthday now, today!' end of message!" He, my brother, called me back later saying he forgot, "work n' stuff" (we're not even married). No, at the time none of this mattered. I'm his only sister having had a birthday on the same date every year, all of his life!

In charge of me and my destination now, well nearly, I did have big ideas about keeping fit. Getting a pass that reduced the amount paid per session at a posh gym, which is a walkable distance. In my mind, visiting the gym a few times a week and becoming a lithe skinny bitch again. In reality it's a real drag and I'm a pretty unmotivated, lazy bag. Oh well . . . I just cut down the chocolate intake. Started out well, it was a 'thing' with Spruce Girl, who was at work and therefore got it paid for. She was quite offended that I wore my walkman the first time and couldn't talk to her. So it wasn't worn the second visit, and I still didn't talk to her. The staff were a jolly bunch who helped me with all the buttons and associated gadgets, on all the exercise equipment, on the first few visits. They advise that you wear a heart monitor so you can judge when you're going to have a heart attack. After lots of fumbling and it's lodged in my underwear with the tab somewhere, I'd leave it as it wasn't falling down—so I didn't know if I was due for a coronary seizure but knew when I was hungry.

I was surprisingly not as unhealthy as I thought. I was more uncoordinated than I thought though. Discovering that my right side is weaker, which made some of the exercises harder than usual. The treadmill was still too difficult, though I did try. I didn't shoot off the end on my backside this time. I was watching people jogging on the machine, it looked so simple. I have found that if I can't imagine it, I cannot do it. I can't imagine walking, I can't follow the sequence through in my mind, so I was asking people "How do you walk?" Spruce Girl offered, after some thought, "Well . . . you get your left leg and you stride . . . then you get your right leg and you stride . . ." "No, no, no . . . I meant the mechanics of walking!" I told her. She nodded, "You get your left leg and you stride, then . . ." My mum and Space Girl tried to explain, "I don't know—I've never thought about it . . ."

I lost the pass to the gym and was still keen enough to find out about and get a new one, on a health scheme thing running at my health surgery. It was intended to act as a 'springboard' into my new healthy life style. Well that was the idea I think, I do know where the pass is this time though. I was teased by the staff on my return. Oh you're back! how long this time? Ha ha . . . One visit I was talking with a young girl, a very interesting spontaneous chat, wrapping up when she simply said, "I would like to be like you." To which I reacted, "No you wouldn't!" I responded to the statement literally; I should have been flattered, I think. If so, oops and Ta!

Getting to know the staff we (Spruce Girl and I), found out that two of the instructors were getting married soon. So I got the date, time and venue written down in my diary. One Sunday just idly sauntering around the local park on a sunny day with my mum. A young man ran up to me, grinning broadly, "Hello Gillian . . ." So he knew me. I let him rabbit on for a little bit then smiled at him, "Who are you, remind me how I know you, please?" He laughed too, he was the instructor who was getting married and his wife-to-be waved and smiled. Reminding me to get some film for my camera. I waited outside the Abbey, camera at the ready for what seemed a long, long time. They appeared, I took a photo, they stopped for the photo session. They started to move again, I took a photo, they stopped. I took some more photos and had to stop myself, I'd used half my film and they were nowhere near me yet. I did get some good photographs which I put into an album that I'd made, with comments, and gave it to them.

I'd been to the market and gone with the flow of a man selling chocolates and sweets, and bought a 'bargain', loads of bars of "Swiss" chocolate with a 'strawberry fondant cream centre'. Bargain! I was thinking as I left trying to carry my bounty. Eventually got them home wondering why I had just done that. Tried one, I was right I didn't like them. Got rid of a box—a present when visiting Teef Geezer, gave the rest to this couple as they were called 'Kiss'.

Mum and I were walking past the local department store—which brings 'Are You Being Served' to mind. It was closed. In one of the window displays there was a really nice wicker work screen. I stopped to look, telling my mum that I was going to return tomorrow. It had been marked down too, now half the original asking price, it had Gillian written on it! Taking the most direct route home so that I wouldn't forget where it was, it was market day tomorrow too, so I concentrated. I remembered the next day, about the screen, where it was and how to get there. Excellent. I was explaining to a sales assistant that I wanted, "That screen in the window." Pointing to the right window as another sales assistant was walking away from the display carrying it. "That screen . . ." "Yes, it had been bought," she clarified, "it's being put away for somebody . . . Mrs Diffin." "That's me!" I whooped, apparently I'd entered the shop as my mum had left.

Space Girl and I were meeting the girls—Lunch Club—and a big car pulled into a designated disabled spot, I noticed and commented that he hadn't got an orange car badge. He got out before us, I was still taking my belt off, he looked fine to me and I said to Space Girl, "I wonder what's wrong with him?" Closed the car door and asked if he'd got an orange badge, going on that he could be fined for parking in the spot without one. He shrugged and carried on with what he was doing. Annoyed by such rude indifference, "Are you disabled?" I demanded curiously. "What do you think?" he snarled. What can you say? We were both quite shocked by this brusque dismissal and Space Girl noted that he was a John Smith's employee. We spoke of writing to someone and telling them of this rudeness. If I have forgotten my badges we don't park in a disabled spot, it drives me mad when people do! Especially if they look OK, having no apparent physical mobility problems. They do make a difference, so think on you may need this space one day. Some of you will find out the hard way—sadly.

CHAPTER NINE

Well, another batch of medical files coming up—I swear I'm ninety-one!

It started with me being happy. I was going to visit a 'new' mate (aka Teef Geezer), I'd arranged transport to and from, timing noted, money, fags . . . and with visits to the dentist, temporarily over, off I went. Very nice, until flossing between my teeth the next day (because my dentist had told me I COULD!), I flicked one of my NEW crowns into a pile of my junk. I couldn't believe it and I couldn't SEE it! NO! Teef Geezer ran in, "Are you alright?" I was frantically scanning. "Are you alright?" I turned and smirked, pointing at a prong of metal, whilst emitting a sad whine. This gesture was to convey my total wretchedness so that he would help me search for it! "Is that it?" he shrugged, with a puzzled frown. Somewhat dampened, by his much too blank reply, I mumbled, "erm . . . yeah." Crisis over, it was found rinsed off and slotted back into place. I was totally paranoid about waking up and discovering I'd swallowed it in my sleep. But, I didn't.

He went to walk his dog, the phone rang. I answered, "Hello?" My second new crown flew out into a pile of 'his' junk! He's not the tidiest person . . . so, one loose and the other one on the floor—somewhere! It was about the fourth "HELLO?" in my ear that snapped me back into attention. I really was in a dreadful state, I didn't hear a word she said. It was his mum, who knew me, and wasn't at all taken aback. I like her. On his return, he rang his dentist explaining that I was visiting and having a complete oral breakdown. Three o'clock . . . the NEXT day . . . three o'clock! He couldn't understand why it was stressing me so much. Loads of his friends "'ad dodgy teef'." I was beyond 'stressed' next morning, when I couldn't open my mouth and keep them in! I was . . . NOT happy. He walked his dog, I rang his dentist. Three o'clock? I couldn't keep them in my head, I couldn't talk! I was in tears. If I came to the surgery, sat and waited, they'd see me. I sat in the waiting room with a business card clamped between my teeth—it was the only way I could keep them in my mouth! Teef Geezer commented, "You could at least tear the card in 'arf!" Absolutely not, if you're going to do it, do it good! I got in. The dentist asked, "What can I do for you?" I pulled a crown out, and gave it to him. "Oh!" I pulled the other out and gave it to him. Double "Oh." He stuck them back in. My desperation to see the dentist had buggered up my lift back home.

I'll tell you about the original journey to see Teef Geezer. One of my support workers (Stickler), was going to visit friends near my destination, so it made sense for her to drive me down. So she did; her friends were expecting her for dinner, as she was late and didn't know the way to where I wanted to be, she dropped me off at the nearest train station. It wasn't until I'd wobbled, fumbled and closed the car door and then turned around that I was engulfed by a wave of sheer panic. There was a huge flight of steps leading to the station and my support had gone because she was late! With my bag (which was too heavy and too big) and my stick I had to go one step at a time. Fortunately the trains ran regularly and late into the evening. Nothing got broken, I was just pleased to have done it. Nobody else was about and when standing at the bottom looking up, I hadn't thought I would make it, as there was nothing to hold on to.

Now to the return journey. This had been tentatively arranged with Stickler. As she was 'working' by driving me back, the day and time had to be confirmed. Still undecided as to when I wanted to return, I thought about it—if I met up with her when she wanted me to, it meant messing about with the trains and those steps and then paying for the petrol again. Then it was a journey of hours, I'm not very happy on long car journeys anyway. This inevitable 'teef' incident, in my mind, had wasted a day so I decided what to do. To stay and go back on my own, a day or two later. I did telephone to cancel all 'arrangements', giving plenty of notice, and was given a very hard time. Apparently, she'd gone out of her way to bring me down, I was ungrateful and couldn't go back on any arrangements made; they were "...part of my programme..." Annoyed, I pointed out that she was coming down here anyway and I'd paid most of the petrol money, plus she was getting mileage for 'working' with me! Stick that in your pipe and smoke it (She didn't stay as my support worker much longer)! I told her that I was staying and that I'd be alright getting home on the train, alone. Conceitedly and smugly adding that I got here OK! Oh dear! Good move! Stupid! Pride comes before a fall! In the meantime Teef Geezer said that 'we'll go for walks'— hikes!—'see if anything jogs your memory'. Sounds good to me, I used to live here, so off we went.

It started really pleasantly. I was out, with company and it was sunny. After hours (over mountains into ravines etc), my groin was aching. I wanted to sit down with coffee and nicotine. I didn't want to stop and admire the scenery. "Yes! I know it's sunny but I want to go home." I asked, "Are we nearly there yet?" "Just round the corner." he said positively. Oh ... OK. Hours later, round lots of corners, I asked again, "Are we NEARLY THERE YET?" "Just round the corner." I wasn't as calm, "You said that corners ago!" I choked. "Yeah, it's just round the corner!" was his much too relaxed response. At this point, and every corner from therein, I was perhaps a little whingy. I was knackered! I had strained my groin. I wanted to get home. I vaguely heard him, even though I was trying not to physically hang onto him, yet I had no idea what he was talking about, nothing new there really. I had no idea where I was ... yes, I did! I used to live there! Unfortunately, I've lost touch with everybody in this area. We got home, kettle on, seated, fag lit, warm. I was calming. He was freaking about in the background shoving a map up my nose. "We went this far!" tracing the route on the map "... over here, up here, round here, down there." He paused, looked at my raised, 'yeah' eyes. "You did really well! . . . three miles!" Yes, I did really well not to smack him one (I now know that the bad groin means that my kidney numbskulls are awakening and active).

I still had to get home. Deciding to save some money, I opted for a coach journey as far as I could get, then rail and home. Easy. If I didn't 'think', I could do it . . . Usual hassle locating the coach. No problem from here, I wasn't driving. Next step of the journey, locate the train station. I had been told it was 'walking distance from the buses'. Not for me it wasn't; for me, on my own, with a large bag, I had to taxi. When is the next train home? I had ten minutes to locate and catch it. I asked for help, paying with my disabled railcard and, raising my bag and stick, indicating why and how I needed help. I started walking, expecting the agreed help to catch me up and take my clumsy, heavy bag. They didn't and I missed the train. I was getting into a real state, moreso when I found out that the next, and last train home, was two hours away. I threw a very childish wobbler. I was upset, how could the 'help' not have seen me? what, was I moving too fast? OK, so the stick IS a bit dull!

The British Rail staff rang my dad. My brother answered and said that, if I caught a train so far, somebody would pick me up. Well it wasn't ideal but at least I didn't have to sit around for two hours, finding the shortest route between filling and emptying my bladder. So, the train was boarded, for two stops. Then nearly home! Nightmare over! The train stopped as the lines changed for another train. The other train passed, our train stayed stopped. The lines had jammed—the wrong way. It gets worse! The driver came and told us that the nearest engineer was two hours away, but he'd been called! Where's the buffet for coffee? There were two cars on this train and one of them wasn't a buffet car. I took a cigarette out of my bag, lit it and inhaled. Pointing, with the lit cigarette, to the smoking penalty sign and uttered a smoky, "Fine me." Brilliant! "Fine me too!" "And me!" "And me!" My car was full of smokers chatting. We discovered that this hitch, we were suffering was now a daily occurrence. When was British Rail 'fixed' and why? Was it broken? Money?

Anyway, a bus was laid on to take us to the next stop then mine, then home! My mum had been waiting for an hour. The tannoy hadn't announced the delay so she hadn't got a clue what was going on, or where I was. We were both sporting massive grins when we saw each other and we eventually gave up trying to outgabble each other with explanations and questions and just hugged. In my place, my things, my bed . . . oh, it was GOOD to be home. Nightmare over?

I woke up a few days later at half past eight, went for a wee, went back to bed and felt uncomfortable. Nine o'clock, I crawled to the phone, I called my support worker in tears, I was in dreadful pain and didn't know what to do! with myself either! "Call the Doctor! I'm coming now." she ordered. Oh yeah!—I never thought of that! Made an appointment for half past nine. By this time the pain was so bad I couldn't stand up, sit up or lay down. My support worker had to dress me. She chose what I wore (Reminding me of a school teacher we knew to be colour blind. You could tell when he'd rowed with his wife. Well that's what we as teenage fashion gurus concluded. He probably thought he looked cool. His wife stifling giggles, "Yes, yes dear that's the green one!").

My support worker rang to ask if the doctor could visit me instead. Three in the afternoon? Oh . . . No. On the way to the surgery, I accused her of locating bumps to drive over on purpose! She was at the reception, I was fidgeting painfully round the corner, "Hurry up, hurry up." The doctor asked, did my groin hurt? No, it was OK now. I was given a painkilling jab, and went to lie down. Half an hour later, I was sitting up, chatting and drinking tea, to encourage a urine sample. I really haven't got a thing about doctors, even though from my medical file(s), you would guess that I'm ninety one and a bit of a hypochondriac.

I was doing my sample (which looked very dark—because it's IN the toilet! and the lighting is poor. Tut!), got it into the light where I could see it. Oh brilliant. Bright red. Bloody marvellous. What now? Kidney stones, evidently. Excellent, one kidney is making bricks, because it can. Had to go for an X ray, to confirm the diagnosis. Yep! the X-ray showed two stones in my urethra—which looked like grains of sand. THAT'S it?? I had to be dressed for this? Something else showed but the doctor couldn't be sure, ". . . if it was a stone or a calcium deposit." I had to go for a scan to make sure. Hospital, hassle, transport, support. I had the scan, which was clear. I had the most appalling weekend. Fortunately my mum was staying with me and took me to the emergency doctor one night. He prescribed Pethidine. He also told me and my mum that, apparently, the pain from kidney stones was worse than childbirth. At this point my mum almost shoved her boobs up her nose, muttering, "I don't think so." We couldn't argue. I was her first child, born six weeks early, two points off a blood transfusion—my mum's blood is positive, mine is negative—I was born bum first, and whisked into an incubator for the first month of my life. When I was released was the first time she touched me. She would stand behind glass, wondering what she'd been in labour twenty four hours for, and cry when they took blood from my heels. No, I couldn't argue.

But, this was bloody painful, the worst pain I'd been in. More X rays, more doctors' appointments, a visit to the kidney specialist, which meant another trip to the hospital. This time for an IVU (intra-venous ultrasound)—you take loads of laxatives to clear your bowels so they can inject you with dye and it doesn't take days till they can follow your kidney in action.

My friend and support worker sat chatting and drinking coffee. The technician couldn't tell me but it looked like I might have a stone— outside my kidney. He was right. I had to see the 'kidney' man, who, in my opinion, was rather stuffy. He wasn't made privy to my favourite joke—no matter, I was telling it to everybody else. This is a habit/ routine that I've developed, single handedly. If I've remembered what I think is a brilliant joke—I tell anybody. To be branded inappropriate again. Whilst waiting to see him, I spotted a friend. I stood up and waved. He didn't look up. Still standing in the middle, of the hospital waiting area, I waved my arms around to grab his attention. He didn't look up. PSST! He looked up and smiled. "You are the only person here that isn't looking at me!" A bewildered woman sitting next to my support worker asked, "What IS she doing?" My support worker answered, "I don't know!"

They would try lithotripsy. Your stone is blasted with ultra sonic sound waves, which should break it up into bits. Small enough to pass in your urine unnoticed. Another day trip to a hospital, loads of preparatory drugs again. When I got in the ward there was a woman, who'd just had it done, asleep. I was told not to eat or drink, there would be tea and toast on my return. A second lady appeared, it was my turn. What was it like? I asked. Lady one, still half asleep, said it was like being flicked with an elastic band. Lady two agreed, it was like being flicked. Hey, I can handle that! You have to lay on a bed that has a well filled with gel. Hence your kidneys are effectively in this gel, then the stone can be located under and through the bed/gel and bombarded with the sound waves. It's all clever stuff! Gone, thankfully, are the days when surgery was the only answer. Firstly I'd had to have more X rays as they had misplaced the originals. To do this they had to know when my last period was, to make sure I wasn't pregnant. I couldn't remember, but I wasn't pregnant I assured them. My periods, I explained, were strange right now. On off, off off, on off. They had been like this for a while, and I repeated, "I'm not pregnant!" No, they couldn't do it without authorization and signatures. Look, I may be brain damaged but I remember how babies are made. I'm not pregnant. They asked my support worker if she knew when my last period was and if I might be pregnant! I was really annoyed at this point and had to sign a consent form. More paper for my file. I'll probably die of radiation poisoning, but it's OK as I consented. Now, back to the reason I am here! I had to balance on the edge of the bed and lay in the gel, while a ledge was raised to accommodate my, by now, dangling in the way, legs. Because my balance is dodgy I couldn't do this. I couldn't balance on the edge waiting for the ledge to be raised. Which meant I had to slide a little further back. Which meant I had to sit in the well of gel, had to! Those women were right, it was like being flicked. With barbed wire (with my knickers glued to my backside with gel), for half an hour. They couldn't do any longer, I was told, "No they couldn't!" The technician also didn't tell me that the stone wasn't actually in my kidney, so it might not have worked. It might have cracked it! Oh good. So I may need this again! Oh good.

Back on the ward I reminded the nurse of the promised tea and toast. When it came, lady one, with eyebrows raised, "Can you have tea and toast?" I asked lady two if she wanted some too. She shook her head and wrinkled her nose. "Go on you might as well." I reasoned. She smiled and nodded and looked at the nurse, "Yes—please." I said, "This kidney shit's awful isn't it?" and probably offended them both. I asked for more toast and tea for me and got some for my support worker. Well if the going's good . . .

My support worker insisted that I, "Stay and rest a while." Why? "Because it says you've got to!" She said jabbing poignantly at the bumf about this. "I feel fine, let's go." A nurse, hovering, got dragged into this. My support worker, needing support, asked her, "What do you think?" Yes, I should stay. So I had another cup of tea. Then I wanted to go. I'd stayed, and now I wanted to go. I felt fine!! We left, under protest. I was in pain again, the lithotripsy must have disturbed the stone and knocked bits off I thought. So I took the Pethidine. I had to. People around me were very concerned. I had lists all over the place, what drugs to take when, and what drugs I had taken when. Dodgy. I had to keep taking them for five days. I was staying up till three in the morning so I could take my next hit. I'm not sure if I needed to that badly anymore.

One day, under the Pethidine influence, I fell into a coffee table, fell off this onto my straight, upright, wire shoe rack. This is now a lovely 'C' shape, leaning over so much that it almost doesn't stand up. It's alright, if you don't touch it, or take shoes off it. Mallard duck slippers do go with everything in my wardrobe. Uncanny. The table was totalled, flat, dead. I was jarred and scratched but OK. That's one way of getting rid of a redundant coffee table.

I woke up one morning to go to the toilet. My next thought, 'How did I get here?' I was kneeling on the floor. I had fallen from standing upright, straight onto my knees, no hands. What? How? I thought. Then answered myself, "Shit . . . that hurt!" I still needed a wee so I HAD to get up. I was surprised that I still could, I thought I'd broken my kneecaps. In the morning I had two perfect black circles on my knees. My mum called, I told her. She was horrified, and said so, because I had planned and was determined to go ahead with a day out. But it was up to me. Yeah! I made an appointment with a doctor. Note, not 'the' or 'my' Doctor;—'a'—as in 'my entourage of medical minds'. I think I've got a man for each bit of my body. Not the doctor that I'd been seeing about the kidney up to now, who wasn't my head doctor at the surgery, who wasn't my head doctor at a hospital, I tell you . . . No I didn't want drugs, I've got loads of those—and I take them! I then paraded my knees, shoved some literature, from his waiting room, on drugs up his nose. "Pethidine is a synthetic form of heroin." I quoted. I couldn't afford to be a junky. I told him of the squashed coffee table, and said that I couldn't handle this anymore, basically.

The next day the hospital rang, my follow-up appointment for the 'stone-blasting' had been moved forward to tomorrow. I had to call them back to say, "Yes, I'd be there." My two support workers were off on holiday at the same time, how would I get there? I rang my dad at work. He would take me, of course. This meant him taking the day off work for one appointment, I wasn't too happy about this and explored other avenues. My support worker had to come back and support me, the clucky mother hen one (By the way support workers are meant to 'support'—assist me in areas, physical and mental, that are still wobbly and slow). The other one was in Spain.

Off to hospital, it was nine o'clock. I had my kidneys X-rayed again; went to see the kidney man. The stone (felt like a brick) had moved further down. I was to be admitted for surgery that afternoon. Whoa, what? I could have one last cup of coffee now, then nothing till four o'clock-ish! Whoa, what? I had my last coffee whilst they searched for a bed. The 'kidney' ward was full. My mum and dad were called, hey guess what? Your daughter's in hospital again.

I found my room, and the smoker's room. Coming out, I collided with a friend, and his support worker. Hello?—he'd come to visit! The grapevine was in action already. We all did a U-turn as his support worker smoked also. They'd got to the hospital and had to find out where I was. She's not on the 'kidney' ward? They were asked my age,— which they didn't know, they've never asked! They found the ward but couldn't find me. 'She'll be in the smoker's room.' There I was!

The first doctor that I saw took a blood sample. He left the most amazing bruise, that clashed with all my track marks. My mum came first with pyjamas, dressing gown and toiletries and found me in a private ward. I got changed and had my pre-med. I was lying down drifting and complained of a severe headache. I was given pain killers. I shortly complained, to my mum and support worker, still there, that at nine o'clock this morning I had felt fine! I could not believe how totally dreadful I felt now! I'm going to be sick! Lots of fumbling. I threw up, lots. "See—told you I felt horrid!"

My bed, was filled with air to relieve/prevent bedsores and in a private ward. There was a continual beeping. Mum and I scanned the room. TV? No . . . Light? No . . . Heating? Still beeping . . . My support worker came back and said it was the bed! She pressed the mute button. It measures pressure, so the pressure must be wrong. I didn't care, it was sorted— quiet now. We had intermittent beeping from hereon, but explained them away and muted them.

Have you had general anaesthetic? I was looking forward to it. My mum and support worker stayed until I went to sleep—that's the only way I could get rid of them! The anaesthetist was getting me ready. I felt that I should say something. There was a space that needed to be filled. So I filled it:

> "This guy has a steering wheel in his fly. He goes to a bar and the barman asks him, "Did you know that you've got a steering wheel in your fly?" To which the bloke tuts, "I know, it's driving me nuts." I heard my mum and support worker groan, and laughter, "That's a good one!"

My mum says that it was really scary. Apparently my eyes stayed open after I'd been injected with the general anaesthetic. "Is that it?" she asked. My support worker comforted her, "I think so." Then my eyes closed slowly. I vaguely recall coming round; well, I remember that the male nurse was good looking. I don't remember going back to the ward or if I slept. I do remember that my dad and case manager were there. My dad also brought some kit for me. We all chatted and drank tea. My first drink since nine o'clock that morning—nice. My case manager went off somewhere to let it be known her feelings on the Pethidine. She'd already told us—a few times. She was appalled that I was taking so many and thought I'd Over Dosed! Hey I felt fine.

My parents took me, by wheelchair, to the smoker's room, against their advice. I took a few lungs, then wheezed, "I'm going to be sick." Panic! My dad gave me a clean white hanky, I was shouting at my mum that the toilet was "just outside the door!" Well, we were in the smoker's room, therefore I'd passed it a few times and knew where it was . . . Unfortunately, my mum didn't, and ran with me straight past it! I shrieked "No!" pointed behind me and promptly threw up. She was tutting and grumbling as she tried to swing the chair round, and I was sick again.

I hadn't eaten all day, I hadn't drunk either! Why then, when I'd done it all, was I pushed back to the ward looking like I'd been swimming?

The only thing that had passed my lips since early morning had been a cup of tea, which was now smeared all down the front of a clean, white, fluffy dressing gown. Fortunately I'd got a change of dressing gown, unfortunately it was the skinny blue reserve. Isn't it a real bastard when your parents are right for a change and you've just thrown up all over yourself to prove it to them?

Visits over, I wobbled down to the smoker's room. Overjoyed that this dressing gown remained unsoiled and dry—I lit up another. I asked, "Why do my calves really hurt? My walking's crap enough." 'They had your legs in stirrups, so they could insert the camera." Oh . . . I'm glad I was asleep, what a sad image. Bed time! Got warm and comfy. The bed beep went off! Woke up, tutted, clambered to the end and muted it. Must have had my arm wrong or something. Got warm and comfy. The bed went off! I groaned and clambered to the end of the bed to mute it—again. Must be my head? leg? arm? Got warm and comfy. The bed went off! I almost fell off the bed muting it. Got warm and comfy—this routine is taking no time now almost auto pilot! The bed went off!! It'll turn itself off in a minute. No, it won't! In a minute! NO IT WON'T! Eventually stumbled to the nurse's station, "There's something wrong with my bed, it keeps BEEPING and it's driving me mad." I was choked. A nurse came, the pressure was wrong, it was reset. Beepless.

The next morning awoken by my light, "Good morning! Cup of tea?" Seven o'clock, SEVEN O'CLOCK! Why do they do this? So early?

The 'stuffy' kidney guy came to see me. He spoke to my forehead, but told it I could go home. Good, I was a bit fed up here. I got a message at half past ten that my mum would pick me up after work. Hours! I had four cigarettes left! Went to the smoker's room. Told my joke to a few more people, two fags left. Killed more time with lunch when I got back. My favourite—cold hospital mince! Airline packet ice-cream dessert. I don't like ice-cream that much, but ate it anyway. Only smoked one cigarette, one to go. Kill time . . . Started writing a letter—third start to the same person, which I've misplaced—watched some TV. Had my last cigarette. Told someone my joke, for the third time probably, went back. What now? I'll try sleeping to kill time. It worked, I opened my eyes and my mum was there. Home!

I've been here before. Alarm bells. No, stop being irrational I told myself, mum is driving me home! Home head on, you know what it's like! "Where do we go? I think your dad drove this way." Oh oh . . . She'd followed my dad home last night, in the dark. Him, being a clever clogs, knowing all the back routes. She found and followed all the right roads, and then missed our turn off on the MOTORWAY! Can you believe it? I had been here before—I'd got my home head on.

The surgeon had told me, "That the stone was too large to pull down, or break up." So they pushed it back into my kidney and put a stent, (plastic tube!) in my urethra to stop the stone going into it again. My kidney numbskulls are going to be a bit naffed that their brick was rejected—then blown up! Then the stent still has to be removed. More general anaesthetic. Oh rats! That is months away though. The stone blasting machine is so expensive that the hospital has to rent it, once a month, and I am not the only person with kidney stones.

So, watch this space.

I found out that the day after I was discharged, a convoy of visitors had been arranged, via the grapevine. So I missed the visits, cards, flowers, chocolates . . . Oh well, I'd smoked all my fags anyway. The second lithotripsy appointment came through, much sooner than anticipated. Trips to the hospital are becoming routine. My support worker and I don't need directions any more, we know our way around the hospital now. I just follow her. We're getting to know the nurses, the porters, the kitchen staff—Oh no, this is a different hospital. Or rather the nurses are getting to know me, the toast and tea were ready and waiting on my return.

The kidney consultant was, surprisingly, doing the 'rounds'. I saw him on the ward before my lithotripsy and after. His 'sidekick' was off sick. He smiled, twice! I saw, on the monitor screen that my 'brick' had been broken into three bits. The 'bits' were all larger than the very first 'grains of sand' which caused the dodgy Pethidine infusion. I was a little distressed. Two weeks later I had an appointment to see the kidney man. Yet ANOTHER X-ray, to compare with the 'first', and therefore see the state of play, as it were. I saw the X-rays and was rather surprised that the stent was so long. About twenty centimetres long. I also saw that two of the bits had GONE. I hadn't noticed so the stent had worked. On the new X-ray there were definite areas of darkness. NO, please, nothing else! I asked the consultant what it was He looked at me and raised his eyebrows, "Poo!" Faeces? Waste products? Used food? Excrement? In the silence during the drive home I kept sniggering. Spruce Girl, driving, kept asking, "What's wrong? Are you alright?" I'd answer, "Poo!" and she'd almost crash the car.

I was to see the consultant again in two weeks, to have the stent and remaining lump removed. "Ninth of December, alright?" he asked, with his diary open. "That's my birthday." I replied. I'm going in on the eleventh, that's in two weeks, it should therefore be sorted for Xmas. Yes! Only one other thing, I have to give them a forty-eight hour sample of my urine then they may be able to tell me what the stone is and why . . . As you can imagine the containers for a forty-eight hour collection are quite large. If I go out during these hours I have to take them with me. Now imagine if you will that I'd have to FIND the toilet, get there and perform the bathroom scenario. Carrying the specimen around with me all day! 'Adding insult to injury.'

A simple life at this point would be rather tedious. My support worker and I wandered off and were on the point of leaving when I remembered that I was going to ask why I kept dribbling, almost full flow, every time I have a wee (if the toilet's upstairs, I'm almost naked by the time I get to the top in preparation). Slapping my support worker verbally, she was the one who had forgot to remind me. She had no excuse, how could she, it was very important, my laundry basket is full of wet knickers! I stayed outside the hospital for a cigarette. She went back in to drop some medical paper work off at the appropriate department. On her way she called by the consultant and told him that I was making her life very miserable right now as WE forgot to ask. No, I forgot to ask, she forgot to remind me (picky, picky). The answer made sense, my bladder control was totally crap due to the irritation caused by the foreign body (stent). Of course my disability doesn't help. I can't run to the toilet, when 'needs be' as it were. It's no longer a case of, 'STOP IT!! we're not there yet!' Then try not to fall over as you swing round to sit down, whilst trying to undo yourself and remove your lower garments before you wet yourself. This wasn't happening often enough.

Of course the sample ended up being done on my birthday—didn't want to go out anyway. I'd found and made excuses as to why it couldn't be done all week until the only day it could be done, to take it with me to the hospital as requested, was my birthday. OOPS! I didn't think of that!

The kidney fiasco is almost over, so watch this space no more— hopefully. It's happening tomorrow, the finale. Trumpets and fanfares will be the order of the day, this has been unpleasant. I'm going to take all this bit of my book with me. Then, on completion, Dr Kidney Man will have to buy the work to read the next instalment!

On a main ward this time. A people ward! With silent beds! There were four other women, I was the happiest to be there—people!—and I was the only one not in pain! A nurse came, checked that I knew who I was, and put an identity bracelet on me so I wouldn't forget. I'm starting a collection! they're all green and white so far. A young doctor came to see me. We all went to a side office. He sat, and gesturing to a near chair said, "Take a seat." I remained standing (because I could), declining the seat with thanks. Who was I? I repeated my name, date of birth, address, telephone number, next of kin, knicker colour. "Gillian, sit down." mumbled my Spruce Girl. "Why? . . . I don't want to." I was glancing out of the window and he was telling me what they were going to do. "I know." I told him. Then told him in detail, everything that had happened, concerning the kidney, from start to now. Then what was going to happen later that afternoon. A distinct silence, with Spruce Girl gabbling in the background, he slid his glasses up the bridge of his nose. Shuffled his papers together, tapped them decidedly on the desk. "See you later then."

Back on the ward and chatting; you meet some really interesting people in hospital. Quite happy, until lunch came. Having not eaten anything or had a drink since eight o'clock that morning, and not being able to do so until four o'clock that afternoon. I decided it was too much—I was suddenly REALLY hungry. Located the smoker's room, it was the same room but further away this time because I was in a normal rather than private ward.

We had just walked through the door. "The Spice girls!" What?? There were two men in there already, both chanting this as we entered. "What me?" giggled my support, having red hair and a big bosom. No, I'm not jealous, my bosoms won't be in my knickers, ever. Alright, nowhere near, EVER! One patient had psoriasis, a skin disorder. He kept displaying his skinny little legs to show me where the medication was ". . . burning off the good stuff!" By the fourth display it was really bothering me too! I turned to his mate, who was off his face, saying, "If he shows me his legs one more time, I'm going to have to punch him!" We discovered that on the patient's discharge he would be homeless. He was also homeless before! Not a repossession . . . No, the DSS will get involved, they won't let that happen . . . I'm sure? I convincingly argued from my backside. My support worker had to go soon and had started to twitch uneasily, I went back with her. Another woman had arrived, making five of us.

Suspected kidney stone, a young mother who was desperately missing 'her girls'. She had moved from 'The Oval', three weeks ago. She hadn't been round the York Castle yet but she knew the hospital, inside and out! She'd moved up here to live with and marry her man. She was "Desperately missing my girls." whom she slept with every night. She and her new beau were going to try for a baby! "This is a frightful way to start, but maybe it's good practice!" I sympathetically commented.

There was a big jolly lady next to me, reading. "Maude . . . Maude! . . . MAUDE!!" Shrugged, looking at my support worker—maybe she's a bit deaf or something? Turned back, "MAUDE! . . ." Nothing, no! I started sniggering to myself. One more time, "MADGE!" from nowhere! She looked up and smiled. Oops! She had a clot in her leg and something else. She read what I'd written in this section then, and said it was good. I liked her, she made me laugh. The third lady read this too and liked it. They read it by choice! (. . . kinda . . .). She'd had (lady three) to have part of her intestine removed. She was great, I could talk to her for a long time. Her husband had got bone cancer and may be too unwell to visit. So, it isn't just me! 'When it rains it pours'—it's just too pathetic sometimes! We are having monsoons over here! She'd written and had published, some poetry.

Months after we had met, she sent me this:

> Gillian, with hope. Eyes so clear, Senses alert,
> Hidden depths under the surface! Fear not, the natural forces
> Of God's universe are with you,
> MAY HIS POWER AND LOVE SUSTAIN YOU.
> So glad I met you,
> It taught me many things, How to approach calamity
> And not to pull too many strings.

Nice one!

Pre-med time and I wasn't sick this time but was grumbling with pouted lip that I was, "STARVING . . . I haven't eaten since, forever!" I couldn't believe how hungry I was! It was quarter past four and they had told me four o'clock! I complained. Just imagine what I was like at quarter to five. I was reprimanded all the way to theatre, "Lie down . . . arms in . . ." I was propping myself up, I wanted to see. From the next step, I could see two patients in the recovery room. The woman had just opened her eyes as I was pushed off to the anaesthetist (I'm sure my mum comes as it's probably the only time I'm quiet and don't argue). It was the same man, I knew this as he said, "Hello again!" I smiled, "You've heard the joke then!" "Gillian . . . everybody has!"—mum was still there. "Nuts!" he chuckled, whilst getting ready.

When he was ready I thrust a fist out to him with the instructions, "Give me some!" Explaining that I was STARVING and I had been looking forward to this all day! As my veins were being teased my mum was telling me she couldn't be here when I got back. She'd got night school, she had to be there, she thought it would have all been over by now. Here we go, the louder you scream the faster we go girls, I was injected. Tutting and stating the obvious with indignation, I'm still here!? That wasn't it, "This is it . . ." said the man wiggling a small bottle . . . "the Full Monty!"

I remember coming round. No I don't. I remember asking the nurse what the monitor was for. It showed the amount of anaesthetic still in my body. When this figure got to one hundred, I could go. I watched it for a while, then my teeth started chattering quite violently. A blanket with warm air blown into it was put over me. They were armed, so this must be normal. I vaguely recall that when my teeth chattered the figure on the monitor fell. If this means anything? I have no idea, just noticed it that's all. Don't recall reaching one hundred—(so should I still be there?)—or going back to the ward. My mum was there, she was playing truant from nightschool, so she could squabble with me all night. The first squabble being her reminding me of the last time when I smoked. I hadn't got a change of nightwear this time! "That was last time . . ." I stubbornly retorted. Then we go into the 'I'll do it myself!' routine. I don't need anybody! Which isn't a very good idea when you've just had general anaesthetic and you're wobbly on your feet anyway. Eventually she took me, on wheels. "Spice girls!" They were still there! I answered the question, I'd not long since got back from theatre. An almost audible grumble in the background. He showed my mum his legs three times and I'd finished my cigarette. Didn't go swimming this time, I wasn't sick. Even though there was this ". . . burnt stuff . . ." to contend with.

Back on the ward just in time—cup of tea time. Mum had just finished her tea and the visiting bell went. She kissed me, said she'd see me tomorrow and left. The curtains were drawn around the two beds opposite and they both still had visitors. A male 'snarl' was heard from behind one curtain. 'Maude' and I looked at each other, "?", shrugged and smiled. The couple behind the other curtain went very quiet with intermittent squeaks and giggles . . . no, not in hospital!? (A friend read this and asked, "Why not?"). A nurse appeared, so I asked if I could I have some more tea please? She looked at my bed-side table, "You've had two already!" and disappeared. Then I realized that one of the cups had been mum's! I followed her to the kitchen and told her. "Yes, you've had one already." she stated. I hadn't realized that the National Health Service budget was such that you were rationed to one cup of tea per evening! I irrationally exploded and ended with "General anaesthetic makes you very thirsty!" reasonably justifying myself. Got the tea.

Got home with no mishaps. My troubles all started when I got home, beginning with the laundry basket full of soiled under clothing again. I was slightly incontinent due to all the messing about with my 'waterworks'. As a result I was back on the sanitary mattresses again (Tampons being a waste of space!). It wasn't so bad; I used those skinny, slip-proof, leak-proof, dry and virtually everything proof! alternatives which are on the market today. Advertising does work as I bought a packet, a well advertised brand, and they don't say what absolute fun they are! A wasted advertising opportunity! I'd peel the strip of paper off the sticky part, which is supposed to be stuck to the gusset of your knickers to keep it where it should be (some people mustn't know that without being told!). So, you peel off the paper to reveal the sticky part. Which I then have to peel off my hand, then off my leg, then I'm plucking myself again. To balance, whilst messing about, meant holding onto the towel rail and therefore performing this procedure one handed. After all of this a few times, the towel is stuck. Pulled my knickers up— and it's in the wrong place—it was up my backside. Bugger! in the right position if I wet myself whilst doing a handstand. So would then have to start all over again. By now the sticky stuff is fluffy and not so sticky any more, until it reaches bits it shouldn't be sticking to. There must be a way of putting them on easily, that I don't know yet.

CHAPTER TEN

THE FOURTH YEAR

I've just done the weirdest thing. Making coffee—noticed the teaspoon was badly stained. Result—went through ALL my teaspoons and scrubbed all the stained ones. Prompting me to write this.

I do that often: go to do something, get side tracked, get carried away, then forget what I went in to do. Everybody/anybody does. Not all the time—I remembered to make the coffee. Often the tasks I get side-tracked by are tidying or cleaning—usually I notice a coffee stain somewhere (microwave, cooker, fridge, skirting boards . . . everywhere!), then get all carried away. Result—you've seen it. I do it all. Missing things that I don't or can't see, eg: cooker sides.

Well, I was getting warm and comfy last night. In a well perfect bed, under a feather duvet, feather pillows. I'd been out, come in and bathed and therefore was all scrubbed and smelt nice! Yes! That is one brilliant thing about 'this', the moment I get into THE correct position—that is it. I turn off. I don't dream, (if I do they're obviously too boring to remember)!

My bed time routine is enviable. Brush my teeth, go to the toilet . . . get into bed. Snuggle down, get comfortable and warm, and then turn off. Feather pillows, cotton sheets, a feather duvet, eye shades and a head injury—sorted. How's that for routine? The first and last dream that I remember was whilst I was in Tunisia with my mum. I dreamt that I was in my old bedroom, at my dad's place. I was sitting on the bed rolling a cigarette. In the room with me were my brother, Pathetic and his new woman. The room in my dream must have been much bigger than my old bedroom! Something was said and I jumped up, knocking the tobacco onto the floor. The moral of this dream? Don't strop whilst rolling a cigarette.

Bed changing day, my support worker helps me and always finishes off (alright, makes it then) with all the corners lined up! Bed changing night, the bed is always softer, warmer, smoother. "They're nicer if you make them!" I'll give her that, and promise myself that I'll make it tomorrow! It's 'nicer', a warm, comfy womb. I can see the golf ball of duvet that I will, most likely, be tackling tonight grumbling 'lazy cow!' at myself.

I'm pretty much settled here now in my flat, and am getting to remember where things are and to know my neighbours. I was in the queue at the supermarket and the man behind me said hello. I knew that I knew him and asked him to remind me how. "I live across the road from you." I knew that, and repeated this incident to his wife. "A real stranger!" she laughed. Well he was, almost. The immediate neighbours, in the same house as me, are a good bunch. We all live together well, the only hiccup was that young chap with itchy fingers who disappeared.

Then there's my 'gang'—a group of local children who meet and play outside my house. One of them, when I first moved here, marched up to me grinning and announced, "I know your name!" Go on then, I invited her what is it? "Julian!"

There is an auction section in the local Monday market. I was wandering past this fiasco of an auction one day with Spruce Girl, and I bid for a tandem. Fourteen pounds for a bike that I can't ride—it's for my brother and his girlfriend to go on romantic jaunts! Pushed it to a local bike shop to get it fixed up, and only hit a few people—Spruce Girl wouldn't push it! On a previous occasion, Stickler had to carry a four foot high wicker snake through town (its really a plant pot holder—which is now a clothes hanger). Those bloody Monday auctions, 'sucker' must be stamped on my forehead!

Back at the bike shop, they wouldn't touch the tandem with a barge pole! Both tyres were dead, no chain, no gears, no brakes and it was two bikes welded together! Oh . . . Gave it to my neighbour's kids to do up. It's still under the stairs—an eyesore getting in the way—I should throw it away really. The latest news is that the kids have agreed to bin it—but it's still there.

My final visit (to be detailed in this book) to my head doctor at the hospital. Spruce Girl drove me, and HAD to come in with me as my case manager insisted—"The doctor needs to see somebody nice?!?" Still no beard and I noticed for the first time that he is rather nice. He said I looked better and asked how I felt, regarding the epilepsy drugs, "If I had to use one adjective, it would be I feel 'smoother' physically and mentally, but I'm still experiencing petit mals." The daily dosage was raised so now I'm taking millions and I'm still incredibly paranoid about them.

Joke time! Spruce Girl tutted and rolled her eyes "You can't swear in front of the doctor! She's always doing this!" Looking at the doctor who was agreeing "Yes, I remember." he laughed. I told the 'parrot shooting' joke, he laughed again. I turned to Spruce Girl with raised eyebrows—excuse me. He would see me again in March 1999 and would look forward to it, he liked me now. I had a question, "Can I do a parachute jump?" He raised his eyes to answer, "No." No flowery medical explanations or reasons given and none were asked for, I liked this. "Happy New Year!" I said as we left. Making the appointment I asked the receptionist if he was married? "Happily with two children." Oh well. Another Mills and Boon abandoned.

This was the doctor who advised me regarding the epilepsy drugs, which I'm bothered about and had a lot of questions and was really unsure about taking them—self denial—not wanting to admit that I had to. "What have you got to lose?" he asked. Good question.

Another appointment, another day same Doctor. He asked what happened to my periods. I explained that after the accident the monthly thing stopped and started again months later, then stopped again. The monthlies are becoming annual. They were going to test me for the "menopause" as yes, I'd been 'tomato' faced hot a few times. "But I'm in my early thirties! Menopause!?" "Women can have their menopause in their teens, anyway think of the money you'll save on tampons!" He laughed and dropping the tone of his voice added, "Gillian that really is the least of your problems." True. This allows me to neatly bring in my other fave Doctor at this surgery, who I'd had to see when I was weeing red. So he ended up being my kidney Doctor, at the surgery. I had an appointment with him and Spruce Girl was going to take me. We had some time to kill, enough time to go blackberry picking! The piece of land near me has loads that were ripe and begging to be picked. I love blackberry picking, the actual doing of getting that unreachable huge blackberry. You have to get your arms shredded, part of the deal. So, we were out, and I was getting carried away as usual. Reaching too far for THAT blackberry, I stepped on something threw myself off balance and fell over. Spilling some of my labours, and sitting on them. Whilst on the floor I spied loads of bigger blackberries . . . "Hey!!" and picked them. We put some wind blown apples in the bag too. I'd already got lots of bags of frozen blackberry and apple mixtures, so I took them to the Doctors with me. Asked if he liked both, and gave them to him.

The next time that I saw him he told me that they had made a crumble, which was yummy, and he thanked me again. By the way, I kept having to buy packet mixes to make crumble with mine, as I couldn't find a recipe in any of my cook books. Even the 'complete' cookbook, full of weird, clever arty stuff that my dad does.

I have just watched TV, I have to make this comment as I don't watch very often. It seems to be cookery programmes or quizzes on cookery, or quizzes on anything else. I don't like cooking, and isn't the news nowadays horrendous? Everybody seems to be killing each other— including children!?—or trying to wipe themselves off the face of the earth messing about with nuclear warfare. Hiroshima . . . we never learn.

It is my opinion that EVERY country should dismantle their nuclear threats—bar none.

So there. There is already freaky weather all over the world, we are going to disappear under water or all live on Ben Nevis (Scotland). As a world, we know that we have moved on a long, long way, in life changing leaps. Caves to computers. There is no real reason that I can think of as to why this planet shouldn't exist forever—if we stop playing silly buggers. Easier said than done, we are a selfish breed, it's a good job I don't run our country really, isn't it?

Have you seen that quiz on medical matters? Isn't it dire—do you know any of the answers? I've been in and out of hospitals all over the place, the world, and really. Chat shows where the more outrageous the topic, and the more gobby fat American women you have on, the higher the ratings. I'm fascinated that people will go on national TV and talk such garbage.

Have you seen the Jerry Springer Show? The first time I saw it, all the people that came through the door landed one, viciously and heavily, on this poor guy who just happened to be sitting nearest to this door. Is it supposed to be a serious heart rending chat show? The guy that cut off his OWN penis, to deter a real weirdo from stalking him? But, who knows? I have never been stalked, and I don't have a penis. I watched the 'Making of the Jerry Springer Show' and was upset by a scene they kept showing of a woman jumping up and punching another woman who was seated—"Whatever!" with a dismissal hand gesture (mind you I could punch those that do that ALL the time!). She was punched so hard that her head snapped back and you could see the spit flying. I really admired Mr Springer's attitude, his shrugging, if that's what the public want, I'll happily go with the flow, outlook. He's good looking too! bonus.

They interviewed people queueing to be in the audience, who were all going in to watch the fighting. The bigger the better basically, they were all searched before they entered the studio. I stayed up to watch an episode of the real show, that was on next. After an annoyingly long musical break. I too was watching the fighting—with complete repugnance! I wonder why we are fascinated by this?

We are nearly four years 'down the line' now. If any of this reads 'well it's been twenty years . . . .', find me, and slap me, for getting side-tracked and being lazy. My short term memory is still unreliable, my long term is still improving.

(Two goldfish are swimming around the tank. As they do. They pass each other. As they do.
Goldfish one, "Did you know that goldfish have a memory span of ten seconds?"
Goldfish two, "You talking to me? . . . I didn't hear a word you said . . . say it again . . ."
Goldfish one, ... "You talking to me? . . . Who are YOU?").

I'm not a goldfish, any more, all the time. I seem to remember, in the weirdest detail, things, and events when prompted, by someone or something. That are important to me. Everybody does this, I know, but with a head injury this aptitude is damaged or non-existent—when what you had for lunch half an hour ago is a complete mystery.

So one goes on, often detailing insignificantly to prove a point—an "I remember point!" Usually things that have got right up my nose, so far that they've stayed there for a while. I have been accused, heatedly, of remembering what I want to . . . when it suits me! Yep! and being argumentative (a kind way of saying I'm gobby?). Bit of a mental struggle here, particularly when I am right and it's 'in my favour', ie they're at fault. Generally we get one of two reactions. A blank, "It was you you were wrong!" accusation, whereby all my explanations and "Yes, buts . . ." fall on deaf ears. In my eyes, inferring that I'm an inconsiderate, thoughtless, nincompoop. In my eyes I am not. As a result I grumble for a little while, then shut up.

Major eruptions are funny, a sight to see. My mouth gets all worked up, and so does the rest of me—in tune. We can only deal with one thing at once. So if my mouth strops, so does the rest of me. Suddenly I've got two left feet, made of lead, clumsy isn't the word, my mouth follows suit. It's not made of lead—it's full of it. I crash around, noisily. I walk very stiffly and straight legged, my knees don't bend. Then, for effect, I trip over things, everything, kick things, everything. This means black toe-nails again but you can see if I'm annoyed. My brain is so over taxed by my mouth, it forgets how to walk, Come on! This is irritating and it hurts! Walk! or Talk!?

I don't freak and strop all the time, about anything and nothing, I hasten to add! Occasionally this has to be done to dislodge that irritation up your nose. A blow-out is sometimes the only way. People around me respond to these outbursts in predictably different ways. We get what I've labelled, the defensive attack, whereby each argument I present is twisted around, until the accusing 'pointy' finger is bending towards me. I 'stick to my guns' a little while, then get totally side-tracked and forget what I was so annoyed about in the first place. Sometimes months down the line, when it's totally irrelevant, pointless and boring, out of the blue, I remember what it was that was bugging me so much. I want to remember everything I should, important things.

I write things down, as suggested. Things I've GOT to do or buy, important things to say (no, it happens sometimes). I went out and bought, for this purpose, pads of paper one for each room in my flat. Then I bought some more, coloured! pads, one for each room. I was given some, one per room. Brilliant idea! If the pads didn't wander out of their rooms; if, when the paper was found, a pen could be located at the same time; if, I could remember what it was when armed; if I didn't keep getting side tracked. Pen! Often distracted by a splash of coffee on something white. Kettle—this sets me off—microwave, cooker, fridge, freezer, skirting boards, doors, walls . . . ?? pen! This is now a futile prompt. When I have 'de-coffeed' all these things, and more. It's everywhere, except my bed—don't drink or smoke in bed. For obvious reasons. When I can't see any more COFFEE, I put the kettle on.

But coffee spills get me, almost every time. Or birdseed. This doesn't get me every day any more. He stands in it, he lobs it he's very messy. But his mess now gets to rodent invasion level high, before I get off my backside and do something about it. Getting carried away, dust busting everything I can. Until the power quits. The bird throws a total loop, but he can get lost!

The lists sometimes go out with me, and remain snuggled and totally forgotten in a pocket—destined to become a ball of indecipherable, sometimes colourful, mush in the laundry. Isn't it a witch when a tissue appears from nowhere! in a dark wash?

Well, Xmas is here again. The time of year when you do the oddest of things 'because it's Xmas'. Not wanting to admit that its just another cold, grey soggy December. Which will cost you more than the rest of the year put together. But it's nice, isn't it?

**** THE BATHROOM PAINTING **** this is to remind me to tell you about when I'd been in the flat a few months. My dad had painted my front room ceiling—biege—and there was some left over paint which was kept 'just in case'. In case my acrobatics chip the paint off a Victorian high ceiling? What?! in case the paint just falls off? It was kept.

Thinking about it now, I have no idea what prompted this, what image I had in mind, if the idea was created in a bathtime mellow moment. It would be rather arty farty and poetic if I could dazzle you with a reason for this action. But, I can't. I painted a picture on my bathroom wall, the whole wall. Which involved standing and trying to balance on the bath, painting, whilst trying not to get paint everywhere, and painting something I would be looking at daily. Don't know how this was done, I recall it being so immensely difficult that it never got finished, and probably never will. Brilliant! You should do it! It's a face. Started with the eye and went on. It's quite good, considering.

I've just remembered how it happened. Having a bath just now and looking at it, well you have no choice unless you sit at the tap end, I remembered. Another one of those brilliant ideas! The paint hadn't been thrown away and I was itching to use it. But how? Originally, I was going to get each visitor to paint something on the wall. The first visitor drew a symbol. He told me it meant something but wouldn't say. If I wanted to know, I could find out in a music shop. The plot grows thicker. At the time I was terribly intrigued, and irritated with him, as he would not tell me. So much so that I painted a face round it. What ever it means, it's now an earring. It's still there, he has long gone. Fair-weather friend, one of many.

Showing my mum she asked, "Is it a self portrait?" It didn't start out to be, just like drawing eyes and went on! explaining the earring, then eye. Looking at it could be seen where she was coming from. The squiggles above the eye could be interpreted as hair, or the mass confusion upstairs. Think I wobbled when doing the nose, it's a bit wonky. Nose out of joint? Her lips are symbolically tight, I painted them small on purpose!

I had absolutely no memory of this painting, done in 1992. The friend showed me this photo when he saw the bathroom in 1997. SPOOKY.

When I was training, teaching a class of four year olds, I was totally perplexed by a boy's drawing book. "Tell me about your drawings." as each page had a black circle with lots of black 'legs' "Spiders playin'." on about six pages in succession. Somebody had obviously suggested that he draw something else! Green was mummy and red was daddy, he jabbed into the corner, "and a spider!" There it was, a little black squiggle. For this reason I have painted the same spider 'playin' on my wall because I remembered this.

Back to Xmas. My first 'real' memory of Xmas, ie unaided. My brother was less than one. I'm older and so had got 'grown up' presents. One of which being a tray of brightly coloured clear plastic interlocking daisy shaped beads. Being totally absorbed (enough to remember them this elaborately), I didn't notice my brother looming with 'yummy . . .' in his eyes. A hand snaked into the tray, fat putty fingers grabbed a pink daisy, and put it straight into his mouth! "MUM!! . . . He's eating my daisies! . . . mum!!" This is all that I remember about them. But, how many bracelets can you make? My brother didn't bother with them again either. He was into cars.

Being six weeks premature I was, ". . . like a doll . . . tiny! . . . gorgeous!" My brother wasn't. Don't know how I missed him, he was a whale. He had rolls of flesh that had big creases in. Probably because if it didn't move he put it in his mouth. My mum's just read this, "Ah . . . he was lovely! . . . he was just bigger than you! . . . that's all!" Alright—he was just very round then, with feet.

Xmas . . . Know what's really strange? 'Pathetic' came home for my first Xmas like this. I went to see him, alone, the second. I don't really remember this time. The memories I have retained are easy to forget. I recall the nightmare journey, both there AND back and I remember Mr Blackbelt (the husband) punching me—a second Dan, who said he loved me and ". . . marriage was for better or worse . . ." Sad.

It was last Xmas, he said he wasn't coming home, to see his "Babee." Xmas number three. Re-cap: Xmas one he came here, two I went there, three . . . Gobsmacked . . . why not??? 'He said that he, ". . . couldn't afford it . . ." Oh! After he'd put the phone down, I woke up! Hang on, he's in the Middle East, his rent and flights are paid for, petrol and cigarettes are virtually given away . . . his only real expenses are food and drink . . . is he an obese alcoholic? He wasn't sending any money to help me out either.

When he called me, not very often, the conversation was heavily punctuated with the reminder this was costing him a 'fortune'. This bothered me. To tears sometimes.

My mum and dad were driving an Escort and the wheelchair didn't fit very well into the boot. Pathetic saved the day—we didn't notice the white armour was scratched dented patched and rusty. "I'll buy a bigger car!" So he did, kinda. As he was abroad my dad had to sign all the paperwork—all the legal, money stuff. My husband would send my dad the agreed amount of money each month for the car. My dad is quite pleased here, a big posh new toy to drive around in and he wasn't paying for it! Nicely! Two payments, then the next cheque bounced. There must be an explanation! There was. He'd spent it, basically. He spoke to the car people and reduced the amount of cash per month. Then he, ". . . could handle it . . ." Sorted, for two payments. Then his cheque bounced again.

My dad was not so pleased any more. He's now stuck with, and paying for, a car he didn't choose, didn't want and can't afford. And adding insult to injury, the CD player has never worked. Nice one! I'm still a bit sore about this. My dad? He's now very spoilt, he COULDN'T get rid of it (he likes beans—he has to because he can't afford to eat anything else). It is a very nice car, I can't remember what it is!

I needed a computer as a divorce settlement—to get over my trauma. Well I don't drive anymore so a Ferrari was pushing it a bit! Fair play to him, got my new toy. It's a dinosaur, but I'm doing this on it. This will be a satisfying, final 'RRRSSSSPPP!!!' in his general direction, when I'm a hobnobbing, wobbling, novelist. Ha!

What REALLY upsets me, even now, is the fact that, considering I have made astounding progress, he wasn't here. It has been a lonely, frustrating, nightmare, and he missed it. Half of marriages end in divorce as a result of a head injury. I know this but I don't feel that he gave me a chance. When he last saw me he was basically carrying me round. I was on two sticks and couldn't go out without him, falling over with regular monotony. I still do (fall), but as a percentage it's much reduced.

So, Xmas is here—(I'm back to where I started, before I recalled Xmases past). Is this a widespread enigma? The all or nothing syndrome? When you are sat at home tapping your fingers for days on end. Then you get two party invites, wey hey! On the same night. Then you 'um' and 'ah' and have to let somebody down, when you hopefully opt for the happening party.

Option one, which I'd committed myself to, a group of people who I see weekly. Lovely people, who are going to read this, who are—give or take—ten years my senior. Choice two, friends that hadn't been seen for ages—fellow headbangers—and their 'support' workers. I'm middle aged in this collection. Telephoned, uncommitting myself from option one. So, out for a curry. Don't like them that much, but hey! could have something else. Got my party togs on, the mini skirt—again, well it's worked before! and off 'partying' we went.

Mr Married Man: "You've got lovely legs. They've given me a stiffy!" Ta. That's all very well and good, but they don't work! "You're a bit of tease really, aren't you?" he explained. Yeah right, so I've got to dress like a boy so you can keep your 'teased' hormones under control? "I dress like this all the time!" was my indignant reply—well he was a 'bit' of a guinea pig on the skirt front, and it worked. Yes! Well, I have got nice legs. If you've got it flaunt it? It was a mini mini skirt. He had no chance. Bloody hell! anything for attention! Still. It's just the legs now though . . . and only if I'm seated. If I stand or walk—they go all weird! and take the rest of me with them!

A man who happened to be married played an educational role in my life for a short time and checked out my computer for me. He visited a few times, then a few times more and kept delaying the departure. A mutual attraction that I was becoming aware of. He makes me laugh, which is important. Actually, that's IT! He makes me laugh! But, it's because of this I enjoy his company. An interesting chapter, is the book closed? Who knows? We're not dead yet.

Bloody jerk, I've just spoken to him on the phone. He was curt, rude basically. For no reason that I gave him. So, I think that I will close that chapter in my book.

When he reads this . . . tart! He knows what I mean! He's turned into a complete weirdo on me. He's stopped making me laugh. I don't know how to play the role of second fiddle, I don't really want to learn. If I sound like a 'spoilt child' here, I suppose that I am where certain issues are concerned. But we all have 'ideals' as far as relationships go. The hassle starts when you compromise and it will be alright . . . if. He was nice, but, obviously not THAT nice—wanting more than a quick poke whenever it suited. I'm nice . . . but obviously not THAT nice.

"Well you never know!" as Teeny keeps telling me. Indeed. A fine theory, until I move or talk.

(We're back at the Xmas curry). There were about twenty of us, clients and their support workers. We were all shown to a long table. I opted for the nearest seat, to me and the toilets. Between two people and opposite one, a support worker who I'd tangled with previously. She exchanged a civil greeting (the smiles not reaching the eyes that were saying 'bag'). One client kept groping my leg and another client was trying to have a conversation with me. Don't know what he was nattering about, I kept being distracted. Never found out—he got bored and wandered off.

Nobody spoke to me. The support worker who had arranged all this was almost doing naked handstands on the table to create a Xmas party atmosphere. He was having a great time. I was making everybody plop their cheap, token, Xmas party crackers. It's OK, the line was drawn at the nasty 'we're together!' hats—well strips of shaped tissue paper that ALWAYS rip (my dad and brother always sat at a very 'proper' Xmas lunch table with hats so torn that they just stayed put. Fat heads). We stand out enough, even seated. Then it was home time. Oops! I think I made the wrong choice of parties.

It was the weekly meeting the following day of the people whose party I'd missed. Therefore party gossip in the morning. Gossip? well . . . the table was FULL of the leftover food. Gosh! there must have been loads I thought. Then, YUMMY! Then found out why there was so much food. Three people couldn't eat that much! Only three people had turned up? This is the point at which I apologised every other sentence for 'letting them down'—in between mouthfuls.

My morning had started badly. One of those mornings when you turn the alarm off, and turn over. Just five . . . You've all done it! or will. So off we wobbled, an hour late. My art file and box, my walking stick and hand bag. The stick in one hand, bag over my shoulder and file under my arm with the box in this hand. Easy.

It all started to go dodgy at my front door. After, irritatingly, dropping each item a few times whilst fumbling with keys, got to the main front door. Frost. Almost wimped out. Shoved my bag onto my shoulder, again, I'd got a taxi booked for the next appointment from (and after) this one. So had to go. 'I can do this!' pushed my bag onto my shoulder picked everything up and off we stumbled (I'm shrieking inside as I type this). To walk without falling over, meant that was all I could do. The art file and, fortunately handled, box are not heavy but clumsy and too large. My bag kept slipping off my shoulder taking my coat with it. To sort it out meant stopping and dropping everything literally. Already being an hour late this was done once.

Got to the end of the road almost naked, just round the corner . . . thought I . . . NO. Do you KNOW where thought gets you? I love cliches; there's one that suits everything. This one gets you across the road, as the footpath is closed! Had to stand waiting for the lights to change so it could be crossed, carrying my coat with my bum, my fingers frozen closed around the art stuff. Crossed, walked a bit, then had to cross back to get to my venue over an hour late. So entered the room, late, cold, half dressed, terribly agitated and apologising.

It was whilst recounting the horrendous start to my day that One was getting side tracked by all the nibbly buffet food in front of me. Well that's what it's supposed to do. Filling the plate handed to me. Three people? Nightmare! Apologised again. At least you called, was the factual reply.

Breakfast!, and lunch! Seated and stocking up, the left over food was being packed away and being scanned by me to make sure nothing had been missed. It had been declared that if anybody wanted anything perishable that was left over then to take it. The lady next to me started to fill a carrier bag with sandwiches saying that if nobody wanted them she would take them for her dogs. Big dogs! The lady that had arranged the food commented, "You let your dog eat white bread? I don't!" It amused me. Still filling the bag she carried on explaining that HER dogs would eat anything! The quiche came next, another carrier bag; her son was a human trash can, he would eat anything too! He must be obese, I smiled. I only noticed and gawped as she kept making excuses and explaining why she was clearing the table. Just take it next time. No, there won't be a next time. People had paid for the buffet therefore committing themselves, and just not turned up. How rude and thoughtless. I thought the lady that had arranged the food was a bit ruffled. Voicing my opinion that she had every right to be. "Why?" I was cut short, "The food's been eaten!" That wasn't my point, tried to explain. "Nothing's been wasted! She's OK!" She's pretty cool, she probably wasn't phased.

Took some quiche, well why not? Even though I knew it wouldn't be eaten—haven't got any dogs. Carefully wrapped a dish of pink blancmange stuff with peaches, it would get all over my art! It didn't and tasted very nice. Got to my art class and the tutor was starving! "I'll be your dog!" She liked quiche so it did get eaten. Two parties and they were both unmitigated disasters, and I could only get to one of them. The mini skirt didn't work. Damn, I hate it when that happens!

Xmas plans were made by my much physically separated family. Myself, mum and dad were all going to family friends (minus my brother). Another first. Oh well, odd but these things have to happen at some time. All my latest 'firsts' leave things to be desired, this saddens me to despair sometimes. The "dodgy teef" geezer called. He wanted to see me for Xmas. He was coming up in a few days. You can't, I won't be here. That's OK, he'd come up 'till Xmas Eve then go home for Xmas Day. I COMPLETELY crumbled when he added ". . . on my own." (with your ugly smelly dog!). The phone call ended with me agreeing to ask my friend, the hostess, if one more could be accommodated for lunch. Really, he doesn't eat much and he's vegetarian! Told my mum, who's met him.

She frowned and nodded, saying with screwed up nose, "No, that's not fair". All or nothing, told you. So Xmas ended up being at my place, my second Xmas lunch.

My place looked great. I'm getting good at this now! My mum and dad came here too. Making four of us. My brother came to drop his gifts off and to fill his own stocking with his gifts from us. My mum had given me six balls of green tinsel ribbon, thirty pence from a car boot sale. Got a little carried away until the only room that was a 'tinsel free zone' was the bathroom. It even got into the communal hall.

I enlisted the help of a neighbour's grandson to twirl ribbon round a shapely dead branch, acquired earlier, that when adorned we weighted down in a decorated box. Very arty farty, it looked nice. Weird but nice. Teeny stated with raised eyebrows, "You did that didn't you?"

It was Xmas Eve: time for last minute shopping. Asked my guest had he bought my mum and dad something? "No I don't know them!" was his indignant retort to which I reacted. It was Xmas, they had put themselves out to accommodate him! It was just a nice, thoughtful thing for him to do. They would have got him something. It doesn't have to be expensive, just a token gesture, I added. He didn't know them!! he argued. "Tight misery!" was my parting comment. He went out with my brother, who moaned that he didn't get some things he wanted as he was traipsing round advising and 'baby-sitting' all day.

The day came, I got some really nice presents. Can't remember what any of them were, but I know that they were nice. Oh yes I do, I remember the gift that this chump paid for because my brother chose it. He bought my mum a tape, music she had been searching for. Weird relaxing massage music, as she'd just done a course on aromatherapy and massage. She loved it; my brother was gutted as he'd found it.

I had bought potatoes, for roast and mash, carrots, turnip, parsnips, sprouts and cauliflower They all needed peeling and chopping for tomorrow. Took all the vegetables into the front room with the chopping board, carrier bags, newspaper and knives. I think that my visitor rather fancied that I was going to prepare this lunch single handedly. No, I don't think so. As he got comfortable, beer and fags, and folded his arms whilst gawping at the TV—I handed him the turnip saying "Peel and chop this." "How?" he asked!! Later on I asked if he knew how to peel potatoes?" Of course!" he chipped. Nice one! passed them over. I don't like doing potatoes.

I was quite happy eating the traditional dead bird and slaughtered animal all crispy and yummy. My mum brought some vegetarian sausages for him and I'd bought vegetarian stock cubes but we needn't have bothered. I remembered when he came last time, went ballistic about my milk, went out and bought himself some soya milk— white water. Then proceeded to eat a whole fish pie, in two sessions, homemade. By me!

My dad took all the Xmas dinner leftovers to do a Keith Floyd, inviting us all for lunch Boxing Day. My dad's one of those people that has the patience to mess about with food, transforming it so it doesn't look or taste like what it is. The table was full of balls of food of various colours and textures. It looked like he'd got a bit of an obsession about balls. The orange ones must be the root veg, the lumpy ones were turkey balls. Can't remember what the green ones were. He'd done this dish of onions and potatoes baked in the meat juices, deliciously memorable. All seated, dad pointed out the dishes containing meat. The obvious slices, the turkey balls and those potatoes. I was obviously rude and gawped at Teef Geezer's very full plate when he answered my dad, "Yes please mate, I like beans." Baked beans!!? I gawped and audibly tutted when they came and he poured them all over my dad's balls. He might as well have done! "These are lovely!" He was pointing at the turkey creations. Erm . . . looked at my dad who was nodding and wrinkling his nose. Didn't say anything. "These are ace!" The devout vegetarian pointed at the turkey again, looked at my dad for parental guidance and he was just non committed smirking, then my mum blurted, "They're TURKEY!" Dad and I didn't say he's eaten two already—neither did he.

I had a bath but didn't offer the bathroom to him, remembering his last visit when he came for a weekend (a week later I had to ask him, "You going home soon or what?"). When he'd been here a few days I had to ask him, call me nosy, why he didn't wash? Did he ever? I hadn't seen him. "He was allergic to water!" was the reason he gave (was that why his feet smelt so bad?—evil!—because he never washes them?). A few days later I queried the allergy, how did he know? what happens? did his skin bubble up, go green and fall off? "It hurt!" was his reply.

He did use the bathroom this time. Didn't ask. Just noticed that he hadn't washed his head. Any of it. His hair was dry and some lunch was being saved (for later?) in his whiskers. Gosh, I can't recall if he had a beard or if he just didn't shave often! How did he shave at all being allergic to water?

Later on, in Xmas week I was sitting being a novelist and I called asking if he would make me a coffee. He sat down, "Where's the coffee?" Arms folded he snorted, "I'm not making it! You can do it yourself, you're not disabled!" Yes, I agreed, I could make it myself . . . but it was quicker and easier and I was busy. It was a favour! Then asked what he meant by I, "wasn't disabled." Fair play I don't use a wheelchair any more, I don't fall as much, I'm trying desperately to manage walking without a stick in company and I haven't got 'dodgy on her pins' tattooed on my forehead! "You get out an' about don'tchya?" "Yes." I was mentally stuck for any other answer here. What else could I say? Didn't want to sound whingey or unrealistic. I couldn't find the fine line between the two. "I can't do a handstand!" Which to me at that time summed up everything, doubly emphasised by the delivery. Sitting back with arms folded he shrugged, "Neither can I." But, I COULD, I used to be able to! I went on that I couldn't stand on one leg, was a nightmare in crowds, couldn't walk in snow, frosts or high winds. He shrugged again. That was it. Red rag city.

I only remember that what ensued was loud and unpleasant, and I seized upon this moment pointing out with select words that since he'd been here he hadn't done a thing. 'Lazy' and 'git' were in there somewhere. I was a bit vexed when I 'stomped' off to make coffee. Wanker! Carried on writing. Then went to watch TV. I had made a large trifle that we had all sampled earlier. "Of course you can have some, you know where it is."

I answered. Then added, I'm not getting it! Coffee time! I noticed that the sink was full of dirty dishes. Tutted, again! Then noted that there was one clean dish, that had been used for trifle. Sitting down I asked him did he wash his trifle dish? "You saw it dintya?" he snarled. Oh Oh . . . Yes, and thanks! but I was a bit confused why had he left the sink full of dirty dishes and just washed his. "They're all yours!" was snarled defensively. You have been using them too! I argued. Now get this, it's quite a feat, he recalled every item in the sink and they were all mine! He'd washed his! Ding ding, round two. This is getting boring now, I shrugged my shoulders, let's go and play scrabble on the computer.

I like playing scrabble with Teeny, only once this particular scenario took place! She came down and we put the filter coffee on, our ritual, and started playing. There was a knock on my door at four in the morning. "What time do you call this?" That was all I heard. It was her boyfriend. Oops! She came back in, "I've got to go up." Then she grinned, "After we've finished this game!" She was probably winning again. The first time we ever played she got a pathetic score minus one hundred and seventy time penalty. That was then, now I have trouble beating her.

So playing with her is fun, with him—it wasn't. I abandoned scrabble and read my book to him. When my willing audience only just had his eyes open, I had to admit that it was getting a bit late, it was three a.m.'ish. I was up at nine in the morning. Quite happy coffee, computer and fags.

It was market day and sunny. At noon I was starting to get fidgety. Looking out of my 'office' window, yeah it was time to surface. Knocked on my front room door and went in chirping "Good AFTERNOON! want some tea?" The air turned distinctively blue. Ignored it, had just woken him up with a flood of outside brilliance. He'd had a lay in! I pointed out that I'd been up since nine. Three hours really was long enough to occupy yourself in one room, doing nothing. Anyway . . . there's a market outside and it's sunny! The air turned thundery purple as he pulled the covers over his head. He was going nowhere, basically. I wanted to go out and this and the language were starting to upset me. "Come on." said I, trying to appeal to reason. The foul mouthing intensified. If he was trying to upset me, it was working. "Go on your own, I'll stay 'ere." "No." elaborating that everything I own is here, this is me; I gestured with my hands, "There is one key and it's staying that way! The only people I trust to stay here alone are my mum, dad and brother." This got him out of bed with a start. Stood hands on hips, head bent forward feet astride and shouted, "You callin' me a feef?" Thunder and lightning at this point, the storm was progressing nicely. Body language expert I am not but I interpreted this as war. I was really upset and really lost. How did this happen? By now he was stomping, crashing and banging around packing his stuff, muttering almost audibly under his breath. So he didn't hear me say that what I'd said was that I only trust my parents and brother. I hadn't said that I didn't trust him.

This was really freaking me now. I called my dad, was he doing anything? What about my guest isn't he around? My guest is packing noisily I answered. Then told him why. My guest was shouting that I'd MADE him stay up till five! "No, it was three and I didn't MAKE you do anything." He was asleep whilst I was reading anyway! My dad asked, "Gillian, what are you doing?" Crying now, "I don't know!" I wailed. One half of my brain was shrieking, HELP!! The other half still catching up, HOW? "Let me speak to him." Held the phone out saying my dad wants to speak to you. "I'm not speaking to no fucker!" That's my dad he was talking about! My dad may have heard this, "He won't speak to you." I relayed. I don't know what to do, this is awful. I was still getting the verbal tirades so I couldn't forget he was there. He was still packing, he must have been packing and repacking I didn't think he'd got that much stuff—certainly wasn't toiletries! All of a sudden he stood facing me and spat, "You pathetic ****!" It's so offensive I'm not typing it. He went.

I had to call my dad back, then I had to call my mum as he'd filled her in. Reassured them both that he had gone and I was OK. Yes I was upset by what had just happened, I was confused as to how. But at the end of that day, yes!! Result!! It was too difficult having him around. Got busy fumigating my sofa bed. Alright washed the sheets. I told my support worker who said "Ah . . . has he called you? Ah . . . Don't worry he'll call soon." "I'm not worried and I bloody hope not." put her straight. So that was my Xmas, onto the new year. Went to my dad's local, my mum came. They seem to be together a lot now they're divorced.

Walked into the pub and immediately told the nuts joke and my newest parrot joke to two men just inside the door. Who says I'm not fast? I did say, "Hi." first, and I DID know them. Well one of them, kinda, vaguely. I was armed, I had party poppers and silly string. Gave my mum and dad some party poppers, knowing that if they were left with me they wouldn't have one at midnight. We hadn't got our first drink but I'd already got two people with the string. My dad tutted loudly, "You'll have none left!" I got somebody else. He took it off me and put the lid back on, "You'll have none left!" Popped a few party poppers, "Gillian!"

There was a teenager, tall and pretty, who looked strikingly brilliant. Not all relevant, but noteworthy! Hair piled high she was wearing a shocking pink dress. No, she was wearing a shocking dress that happened to be pink. It was minute and strappy, it left nothing to the imagination

Midnight struck, everybody is very loud and happy and you start to wish everybody a 'Happy New Year' and kiss them. Sometimes they're good looking! but it's usually the odd balls that shove their tongue in your mouth! It happened again—a one sided snog. When you pull away, yeuch!, why have they always got a smug self satisfied challenging 'yeah?' grin on their pathetic faces? Or a drunken leer? Should be flattered. All or nothing. Giggling, stupid cow, home, ten steps forward, five back, two forward, stop, ten more forwards, three or four back. I was holding onto my mum and dad too! We should have gone home backwards!

It was still the New Year when we got home, so we had another drink. Retired in my old bedroom quite happy. A few hours later I got up to go to the bathroom. Groped at the door blindly but couldn't find the door handle. Getting desperate, needed the bathroom now, still couldn't find the door handle. Couldn't hold it now, still groping, wailed in anguish, my mum and dad came running and released me. Emptied the rest of my bladder on the toilet through my pyjamas. No time or point in removing them, the damage had been done. Thankfully, they saved my dad's carpet. I should have got wise at this point, a major infusion of alcohol really isn't a good idea. I had forgotten on which side the door handle was. Or I hadn't. The door handle was there on my bedroom door in my flat. Oops.

My dad laundered my soiled night attire, when returned he had ironed my knickers! Bless! So that was my Xmas over into the new year of 1998. No contact from Pathetic, I'm not sure if this bothered me.

During this stay at my dad's (I cannot tell you how this happened, as I don't know. I hadn't been drinking!), I fell so badly in the bathroom that I ended up in the bath with my legs dangling over the side. The yelp and crash brought my parents scampering again. I had the most evil bruise on my thigh already and was whimpering accordingly. My dad held his hand out to me. When I tearfully pointed to my knickers, which were round my ankles, my mum elbowed my dad aside. My dad looked confused and hurt, he shrugged. This upset me too. Mum took charge and helped me out, crisis over. Dad made tea, we are British dear !

I was walking to my writing class today and it wasn't raining. Passed the building site, major upheaval, and paused to look. It's really interesting, with the age of science and modern technology, a river/dam has been moved and it's being built over. To eventually become a shopping mall. There are shops closing down and having sales, in the selection we have already, and parking/traffic is already too much for one main street.

If we already know that the ozone layer, that keeps our planet where it is, is being destroyed by gasses emitted by burning fuel, why are we still doing it so much? We already have freaky weather all over the world, are these occurrences incredibly hyped up by the media or, are they warnings? Or are they both? Big Bang? Will it take amazing deals for topless beach holidays, in Iceland in December? Then will every country, with anything to offer, stop being so egotistical and selfish? Not the people that are in charge. Then will we stop kidding ourselves? We are a little island with wordwide competition and World War Two was fifty years ago.

Paused for thought, then noticed that amid all this building chaos there was a waterlogged area, with a tree. There were two Mallard ducks, a drake and a hen in the water preening themselves, surrounded by trash and filth, ah. Totally out of place, don't we all feel like that sometimes? They'd gone when the class had finished. Crossing the road I thought again, so where was the river? Can't remember, it's changing so fast.

And I'm getting old, I remember when there was a river here. I've remembered a time when I was really naughty, I stole a four pence shell from a shop in a seaside resort, when I was younger! It was thrown away, the evidence, when I got home. Don't recall doing it again, well there was the Ferrari . . .

Nobody can say that they've NEVER been 'naughty' EVER. Being naughty and being chastised are part of growing up, and learning how to get the most out of being a human being. This carries on throughout life. Your actions hopefully depicting your age at some point, and being judged favourably by those around you. Those being affected by your presence.

CHAPTER ELEVEN

My last 'holiday' had been when I went to see Pathetic alone, the year after the accident. It was really time for another! My mum and I agreed to go away together. When the holiday was booked we were given a list of options from which we chose 'Quiet room and ground floor'.

I remembered to take my drugs in my suitcase, my mum's suitcase, in my hand luggage and my mum's hand luggage—not that I'm paranoid about them you understand! I also remembered that I'd written all the addresses I needed in my special 'holiday book' which I packed somewhere, and never saw again (My dad was the only one to get a postcard—his was the only address I could remember!). We arrived at our destination to discover we'd been put on the roof basically. It was the noisiest hotel I've ever been in. But it was clean and although most of the staff were badly paid and worked long hours—they were the nicest.

The problem of being on the roof was rectified. The noise wasn't! The guy next door was some head bloke in the kitchens. He had an alarm call every morning at half past six, and he was deaf! The first time this happened we grumbled and tried to go back to sleep. The second time this happened, after the phone had been ringing for five minutes, I literally crashed out of bed and brayed on his door snarling, "Answer the fuckin' phone!" My mum chastised me, for my outburst. "The phone woke me up too, this is the second time, we're on holiday and it's six o'clock—in the morning." I reminded her. "Oh yeah!" and she turned over. Then we got up, we were awake now. One remedy was to push an alarm clock up his bum, then it would only wake him up.

The next morning my mum was on the phone at half past six. "We're on holiday! the phone next door is waking us up AGAIN! it's been ringing for ages and it's six o' clock in the morning!" Exaggeration for effect! That was sorted too, but I didn't tell her off for keeping me awake chatting on the phone. Then there was the maintenance, which involved a lot of drilling and hammering, as they were trying to up-grade the hotel for the coming season. We told our holiday representative (Lipliner)—who had been very understanding and she'd see what she could do. We also asked her to find out, or please tell us, why we paid extra for a bath when every single room in the hotel has one. A shower too, one of those attached to the taps, so that you had to stand in the bath pulling a curtain round. Those shower curtains that are always sticking to your bum, but I don't have that problem any more because I can't stand up in the shower if its in a bath. So there's a positive for you—no more soggy shower curtains stuck to my bum. Aren't I the lucky one.

As my mum was with me, I didn't use my stick after the first day. A few of the English people there told my mum how marvellous I was, and how well I was doing. They didn't tell me. But I'm glad, I probably would have taken it as patronising, as I was aware of the gawps and waiting for the snide remarks. Our fellow hotel guests were, on the whole, fine. With this you get the real extremes, the 'Ah . . .' team or the rude, ignorant people. My mum and I were walking upstairs and I could hear people coming up behind us. Then I heard my mum comment indignantly, "PROBLEM?" to the people coming up the stairs. I have absolutely no idea why this happened; she wouldn't tell me—it was, "Nothing."

There was a lady coming down the hotel stairs on crutches. I wondered what was wrong with her (as people do with me, but I haven't got the stick so I'm 'drunk'. Isn't it shocking, I must be drunk all day, every day—huh?). Like me, she looked all right until she moved. She'd had one of her legs amputated as a result of a road traffic accident involving a cyclist.

The hotel had an indoor pool that was almost too warm, but it was lovely, and like swimming in a bath. For the first week I went in almost every day, although swimming is still a painful nuisance because I used to be good at it. But I did enjoy this pool enough to ask the Tunisian life guard whether he had seen me swimming. Trying to explain, briefly, the accident, I also asked him why did my knees hurt so much. "Rheumatism." he said, nodding knowingly. Nah! Thanked him whilst moving away, and probably splashed him.

There were bingo sessions in four languages, every night. It takes a long time. Each number was said in French, then English, then German and then Arabic. You start to miss the number said in your own language as you think you know them in French. Then check with the English said next if you don't miss it which you often do, or I did, then have to question the number that's just been said four times.

I was taking some notes whilst I was there, for this book, so that I wouldn't forget. Almost like a diary. This is what's written next, 'It's the cabaret tonight, the entertainment staff, all two of them, take the stage. Hope it's the same as last week. Brilliantly funny. It wasn't, but it was still good. They were miming to and interpreting well known songs'. Just thought you ought to know.

There were lots of stray cats around the hotel that hid their kittens somewhere, you could hear them. Either that or the bushes in Tunisia meow hungrily all day! One cat got inside my mum's bag, whilst we were sitting by the pool; it was looking for food. Even when she picked the bag up, admonishing "There's no food in there little cat!" it burrowed back in: "It's in here somewhere!" Another day by the pool, another cat (a tiny thing) picked up my sandal—and ran away with it. Mum and I laughed, then realized it was still running with my sandal! It stopped and my mum got up to collect it. Lo and behold, it picked it up and started running again! Mum gave chase this time. Then another cat joined in, and was chasing the first cat too (it reminded me of The shoe! The Life of Brian by Monty Python). The cats started fighting for the sandal and the first one sorted the trespasser out: 'No, this is my sandal'. The second cat, not deterred and still wanting a turn, started fighting again. At which point all was settled by the long arm of the law (aka my mum). We were sitting out alone that day and so nobody else saw this! An excellent camcorder skit, if we'd had one.

There was a young woman, on her honeymoon, who kept feeding and playing with the cats. She'd got cats at home and, "It was disgusting!" how loads of the cats were pregnant and they were all diseased! They kept sneezing and their noses were really snotty, the cat woman kept wiping them clean! Yuck! The rest of us, including her new husband (oops) were shooing them away. I love cats, but they all looked grotty or were getting that way. In the second week we all had—including the staff!—this really horrendous cold/virus. One of the symptoms was messy sneezing—so we all blamed her!

At our dining table we had a mixture of German, French and English. This made for interesting mealtimes. I knew a little French, mum knew a little German and they knew a little English. Meaning we were all translating for each other, understanding key words and getting a big fat nowhere, although when it rained most of the second week there was mutual understanding. The French man was so obviously focused on me that it was causing gossip, apparently, the question being 'will she?' Well, he was alright. Saw him at the bar and played pool with him and his two boys,(badly)—the kids liked me, and 'chatted'. He took his kids to bed and came back to the bar to carry on drinking with me. He asked if I wanted another drink in his room? Yes! as you do—just one more. When you are that happy you want to extend that mode as long as is humanly possible. Told my mum that's where I'd be, she was not at all happy about this, "I'll be alright!" I 'convincingly' reassured her.

Well, we got to his room, and his children were in bed asleep, sat on his bed with my drink. He sat next to me leaned over and started kissing me. Oh no! I pushed him away saying loudly, "LES ENFANTS!" Then he pushed me so far back he was almost laying on me, this was awful and so was he. I pointed to his kids again. He shrugged. I pushed him off and away from me and left as quickly as I could. What a nightmare. Got the, 'told you' routine on my return. I was a little flattered though until we got to breakfast. There were two German girls, one of whom was looking down her nose with obvious disgust and loathing at the French guy. Her friend, whose English was excellent, told us that he had chatted her up and offered her money for sex! I felt disgusted with him too, he hadn't offered me any money!

Mum and I were sitting on a wall, waiting for friends, and a Tunisian man strutted by, flouncing his hair. Paused turned, and strode past again, staring at my mum. Who was trying not to stare, "He wants you . . ." I said. "Adonis! . . ." mum laughed. He was standing like a model 'not' looking our way. Mum was 'not' looking his way either. Nothing more happened as we left, but it would have been interesting to see what the next bit would have been. He'd have probably just kept standing there, changing poses so we got all sides and angles.

There were five of us on the beach. Me, my mum, Daddy, Mummy— an involved couple—and Sweetie—their little girl. "Don't worry, I'll take care of this! I'm good at this now!" Daddy said as a pottery drum seller was looming and there wasn't anybody else on the beach near to us. So, we were all quiet and left him to it. He was quite good at first, "No, no, no! . . . how much?" he started losing it here, "No, No money!" He tried to regain control, then lost it completely when he added "She holds the purse strings!" pointing to Mummy. Well the drum seller was good and latched onto this. He slyly insinuated that Daddy was a wimp, with his money being controlled by a woman, so he couldn't even buy such cheap drums. That was it! Daddy drew in his stomach, and dragged his daughter into it. "You want some drums don't you Sweetie? To go on your black shelves?" Mummy wouldn't give him any money whispering, "We DON'T want any drums! Tell him to go away!" He WANTED the drums now! A gauntlet had been laid. Sweetie had some money so, counting out the loose change from her furry lion purse, he explained that it was "For your drums Sweetie, I'll give it back to you later!"

Daddy was so truly brilliant at turning the drum seller away that I ended up with two drums as well (for my brother and dad). My mum was rocking with laughter, wiping tears from her eyes, "Thank goodness he's gone! I nearly wet myself!" We went with the same family to a big street market—oh oh. He was in danger of buying some leather ornaments; Mummy went behind him and simply said, "Drums!" He said he could do without the ornaments—he'd already got some excellent drums as some very 'nice' ornaments. I had to be restrained a few times too. My mum spent most of her day saying "NO." It was a good day. I didn't spend anything, well not much, and I was snogged by all these blokes in the market.

Sweetie was entertaining us by the pool, singing away quite happily. After a while her dad suggested that she told us 'that story'! So she did, "Down this dark, dark, road there is a dark, dark house. In this house is a dark dark, room. With a dark, dark corner . . . and there is a goat!" !? "Ghost!" her dad corrected. I liked her version better!

The food in the hotel was very fancy and plentiful. My eyes being bigger than my belly and being a bit greedy, I piled my plate high at the first meal to taste a bit of everything on offer. I then tried to carry it to the table—which was a bit silly of me. There was a trail of food on the floor pointing to my chair, which everybody was slipping in. From hereon I did the piling and mum did the carrying.

The part of the brain that controls bodily temperature, the thermostat, is often affected by a serious head injury—so you feel the cold more quickly than most. As a result I was chilly in bed. My mum rang reception and asked if we could have a blanket. I was just pulling a sweater on to sleep in and there was a knock at the door. The blanket! I was impressed; not expecting it until the next day when they made the beds. I gather that this service is quite usual, but what a lovely thing to happen. Another really nice thing was that they arrange your night attire decoratively on the bed. We had flowers and butterfly shapes, they were excellent!

Mum and I were sitting on the beach and yon native bloke approached us with a basket of fruit. Whilst we were saying "Kline gelt" (phonetic Arabic meaning 'No money—now go away!' I hope), he was cutting up a cactus fruit saying, "It would make us like Michael Jackson!" "Pardon?" We repeated: no thanks. He kept cutting whilst talking to himself about Michael Jackson and offered the peeled fruit to me. Which I took, thanked him, and took a bite. Yeuch! I gave it to my mum who took a bite which produced the same reaction. The man then held his hand out demanding, "Money!" When we laughed and said "KLINE GELT!!" he shrugged muttered under his breath, huffed in disgust and went. This was the only 'freebie' I got and it was horrid and got shoved into the sand. Cheeky bastard!

Another time on the beach a young Tunisian asked if I had a light. He joined me; we were having a cigarette and just chatting, sat near the water's edge. A policeman on horseback appeared on the beach and my new 'mate' vanished. I wasn't going to be paid again—I was meant to be paying this time. By all accounts it's quite common apparently, innocent/stupid girls fall for this attention and get into lots of strife (not with their mums tutting loudly at intervals in the background they don't)!

When changing travellers cheques you had to give your name and room number. I had noticed that my name was spelt wrong on the printed receipt, 'Gilliam'. Told the cashier, who told me to tell them at the reception desk. Where he changed it to 'William'. It took a long time to get to Gillian, I should have settled for Wills!

Trying to dance is a weird experience. If I sing along, making most of the words up, my legs forget what they're doing. We do break dancing out of time for a little while until I get my balance back or just . . . stop! Full concentration, and then my moving portrayal of the music still looks as it feels, stiff, jerky and painful. A complete nonsense when I've had one or two glasses of the 'falling down water', as you do on holiday—being in the bar daily (chatting and avoiding the rain), but it was the only time I wanted to get up and 'dance'.

One evening there was a carbaret act involving knives. A few women were asked to go up onto the stage; I was one of them. There were no stairs leading onto the 'stage'. So to get on it I had to sit on the platform, swing my legs round, get onto all fours, pause, get my balance, and then stand up. They asked me to get back down from the stage. I was really humiliated and disappointed, not knowing what I was supposed to be doing. It was decided for me that I couldn't do it. The volunteers had to stand on this man whilst he was laying on broken glass, or act as weight when he was doing something odd with something very sharp. "If you'd have slipped—you could have both been killed!" mum stated. I couldn't argue, but I still was not very happy.

There was a Miss Hotel competition and the entertainment guy was grabbing unwilling (untanned) women from the audience ("No . . . no . . . no . . . oh OK! if I must!"). I SAW him look away to avoid my gaze. THIS really upset me. In my previous life . . . The entrants firstly had to run around the audience collecting as many kisses as they could. The men liked it. I would have sat on the stage (would have had to) pushed my dress up high then puckered up my lips announcing, "Come and get it!" Then I would have been gutted when nobody could be bothered to get up. I didn't think of doing this till after! What upset me was that I wasn't given a chance to try to overcome the obstacle of needing to run about. The foregone conclusion that I couldn't do it. Well, maybe not like everybody else but still . . .

The weather was horrid during the second week. There were lots of us round the pool, desperately trying to get tanned in the half hour of weak sunshine, only to be sent indoors by a cold downpour—to drink more coffee and sit moaning again—still it was good training for home. I wore some trousers to go on a camel ride—not just because it was cold. The idea was to stop, have a drink, and get dressed up Tunisian village style (charity shops would bin the clothes we were given)! We'd all (me, Daddy, Mummy and Sweetie), laughed with ridicule at the camel my mum was riding on the way there. It kept stopping, crapping and was always on three legs scratching its balls. I got this mule on the way back! It was a real jerky jarring ride which spoilt the day. I started to feel really ill with a violent headache. I had to go to bed when we got back. "Next time we won't go for three hours! Maybe we overdid it!" mum said, explaining why I felt so awful.

The entertainment man in the hotel had organised a Turkish bath expedition. A chance to be too warm! Mum and I went, with no problem hailing the taxi—they are everywhere. You flag a taxi—and three pull up. After the bath you were rubbed down with something rough and kneaded. I nearly punched the guy doing me! The Germans complained bitterly to the entertainment chap who had arranged this, that the experience was too rushed for the money paid, and they weren't rough enough! He turned to us with his eyebrows raised, looking very fed up. We answered him, by shrugging. He smiled.

The last evening, having lost at bingo and done the chatty dancing bit, it was time to retire. The entertainment man came over to say goodbye. He asked how the holiday had been, and chatted about his English fiance. I finished my drink and, still talking, stood up to leave and my legs just concertinered. I ended my conversation chatting to his knees. The up-down motion was so sudden and rapid that nobody reacted. There was lots of confused drunken sniggering as I was helped up, my mum took over and tried to get me upstairs. It took ages, three steps up one down, snigger break, another two. My mum was doing the same after one and a half flights of steps but when the top could be seen, she got all serious. "Come on! . . . lift your feet up! . . . I need a wee!"

At the airport, coming home, we were delayed. Which wasn't a problem until a fellow passenger told us that when this happened to them last time, they were stranded in Tunisia for five days. Their luggage had gone to England and they hadn't, so she always kept a toothbrush and a pair of knickers in her bag! Then someone else told another story; this time it was announced that the runway would be closed for maintenance. They had ten minutes to board the plane, or be here tomorrow. They got the plane, all running and being thrown into their seats. Any seat! "You've never seen anything like it!"—nor do I want to really. It doesn't matter how good a time you've had, how wonderful it was, when it's home-time it's home-time! All of a sudden you want your own bed, your own place and your things! A normality space. It was a good flight—eating and watching 'Men Behaving Badly' and an episode of 'Only Fools and Horses'.

My most recent joke:

> Two blokes hike to the top of a hill. Egging each other on to the top, where one of them puts a budgerigar on each of his shoulders, and jumps. He lands breaking everything and can't move. His mate calls down, "You alright?" Gets the answer "Yeah!" The second bloke puts a parrot on his shoulder. Shoots it! and jumps. Crashing next to his friend breaking everything too. The first chap spitting out broken teeth, "I'll tell you what mate, I don't reckon much to this ere budgie jumping!" His mate pulling his glasses out of his nose, "Nah, this parrot shooting's crap too!"

CHAPTER TWELVE

Gadget Boy is visiting from the Middle East. He was the last person I saw on THE night, and he's taking me to Italy. He's taking me to his niece's wedding first. I haven't been to Italy and I love pasta. Is this book turning into a Mills and Boon ?

This was the agenda: he arrived, the next day we went to his niece's wedding, stay in a hotel that night, then back home to pack all my summer clothes—and the day after that we fly to Italy. I didn't have any hospital, doctor, dental or chiropody appointments. They had all happened in preparation. I was dead excited!

I bought a posh brown skirt suit to wear at the wedding, and very nice it looked too! Had my nails done and they were quite long, so looked good in gold nail varnish. I even had my hair cut! The hairdresser said, as I was being indecisive as to the length I wanted it, "Do you want it shorter, but still long enough to tie up?" "That sounds good." I said, lobbing the ball back into her court. I asked for this, I had to remind myself when I'd washed it myself and COULD NOT DO A THING WITH IT! It's always in my face and too short to stay tied up out of the way. One just cannot eat chewing gum on a windy day and talk— or walk that well— the wind blows your hair into your mouth which relieves you of the gum. This happened a few times before we clicked on to the reason why.

Gadget Boy arrived and looked good, especially when he'd changed into his top hat and tails. I looked elegant—apart from my hair which looked pretty frightening. We had just over an hour to drive into the middle of nowhere following written directions, and I HAD to go to a hairdresser—where they couldn't really fit me in, but if I sat and waited, they'd see what they could do. But when I wailed, all dressed up, "I've got to be at a 'flash do' wedding in an hour and look!" pointing at my head. They fit me in and I thanked them profusely. He went to sort out the holiday insurance, in case I'd goofed. Came back when the transformation was complete and I'd been harmonised and didn't look scary. The insurance was OK, although I wasn't covered for any kidney problems. But I knew that already.

So off we went looking the part. The wedding was elaborate, organised and impressive. But, you had to drive from the church down into the village to use a toilet. Everybody had to keep nipping off as the after wedding photograph session took FOREVER! The photographer kept coming round the guests asking for, ". . . the bridesmaids . . . bride's family . . . groom's family . . . page boy and bridesmaids . . . cousins . . . uncles . . . grandmother . . ." Gadget Boy's mum was being very helpful to save time. "He's over there, she's there, she's by . . . Oh, that's me!" Gadget Boy was mingling and taking photographs of the bride, telling me how wonderful his camera was and what it could do. Again. By now we were all on the verge of lynching the photographer! I should imagine that the photographs will be worth it, some of them have got to be brilliant.

The reception alone was worth getting married for. All the table decorations were in the same tones as the bride's and bridesmaids' outfits. There were matching place name cards, matching menus, each guest got a small gift of sugared almonds wrapped in the right colours, and there were different wines for each course—which was very nice. One of the courses was lemon sorbet to cleanse one's palette. It was so nice that I wanted to eat it all!—but couldn't; it's not that nice after a while.

The evening just drifted in, and I stayed seated. Gadget Boy was wandering around talking most of the night, which was OK, they were his family. A very nice bunch, who were chatting and drinking with me, keeping me amused. If my glass was empty there were volunteers to fill it, so I let them. At the reception I was chatting with Gadget Boy's sister, mentioning the book and telling her that her brother appeared. Under the codename "Gadget Boy!" She grinned broadly at him "She's sussed you man!"

Uncanny.

Bed time. We had to find the room and I was having a nightmare with my stilts which I couldn't keep on my feet. I was alright as I had an arm to lean on—or stagger with! The next morning I woke up, sweating. The heating had been on all night. I was also becoming aware that I felt as if I'd had alcohol intravenously the night before. I was feeling completely horrendous. As I'm rubbish on my feet anyway it's difficult to judge, when you're very happy, when one more is just stupid. Well one's a bit silly really, but there are some occasions—parties, pubs etc . . . when this just has to be done! This was one of them.

So I woke up quickly knowing that I was going to be really ill. Stayed where I was—I'll be alright in a minute. Gadget Boy left the room, I don't know why and didn't care. I'm going to be sick! Got to the bathroom and stood in front of the toilet with my mouth watering in preparation. I was starting to have a complete nightmare! as I was retching something started to happen at the other end. Gadget Boy didn't witness this thankfully, the bathroom door was wide open as I'd only stumbled in there to vomit. I had to sit on the toilet whilst puking in the sink. Sad. We never learn—no, we don't do we dear?

We passed the newly weds as we left the hotel. I didn't recognise her at first, but when I did, I asked where they were going to on honeymoon. The Seychelles! To which I commented, "Nice one—we should all get married!" The woman behind me laughed, "Yeah I'm going to Cornwall!"

We returned to the flat and packed all my summer stuff again, packed all my drugs everywhere again—shades of Tunisia. Everybody I spoke to who had been to Sorrento and Naples were making me impatient to be there. It sounded fab: lasagne, Gadget Boy, sunshine and scenery. At the airport having checked in, Gadget Boy went off to sort a hire car out for our return, to save my dad the journey. He was gone for a long time so I went to investigate. The lady with whom we had checked in came up to me asking what I was doing? My flight was boarding! Oh . . . my . . . God. Explained that he'd gone off and that he'd been gone all this time, and he'd got my money and passport! I was getting a bit flustered now. She took me to the desk and telephoned the flight staff telling them to put our luggage on standby.

I was telling another member of staff that, "I don't know where he is . . . I just don't know!" Crikey, what a nightmare! It was all going too well . . . up he sauntered with a massive self-satisfied grin. "I've got the car sorted!" he smiled and I couldn't care less! Semi-stropped verbally, and therefore physically, until we were seated on the plane. Then he turned and said, "See I told you we'd catch it!" and I could have slapped him—hard.

I had initially been responsible for finding details for the holiday. On the phone he'd asked what the hotel was like, ". . . Pink." "What's the swimming pool like?" "Erm . . . I can't see," I'd said, adding "I don't think there is one, the hotel is . . . just in the middle of a road!" He called the travel agents from the Middle East to book the holiday, and up-graded the hotel! "Do you mind?" he'd asked. The girls were still giggling excitedly when I went to pick up the tickets. "If I come back walking like this . . ." trying to do a John Wayne-style walk, "you'll know a good time was had by all!" My support tutted and rolled her eyes as I fell out of the shop.

So the hotel was nice and had an outdoor, and an indoor, pool. The food had a high rating in the brochure and we were booked for half board. There were lifts and it just happened that our second room door was directly opposite the lift. We found that the first room we were booked into only had a shower and told them that this wasn't of any use to me because of my balance problem. They agreed to change our rooms and move all our things, so we went out. It had been an hour's journey from the airport to our hotel, during which time the rep told us to "Be careful with the local lemon drink! people don't realize how strong it is!" This had to be tried!

Even in the dark we could see lemon trees—everywhere. It was raining but it was the first day. Found some shops! We saw lots of marquetry (inlaid wood of different colours that make up a picture or scene). Gadget Boy and I had our first dispute, he said that this was also known as parquetry. I disagreed saying that "marquetry was 'arty' and parquetry was more geometrical and floors were done in this way. They were both in-laid wood techniques though . . . I think." (I meant to look this up when I got home but it's not bothering me anymore). I wasn't totally sure that I was right but his insistence that he was, and I was talking out of my backside, was irritating after a while and making me walk badly. Would saying, "I just don't know." have been too hard? I did, as I wasn't sure.

(Space Girl read this, and she was bothered enough to look the words up in her dictionary. I was spot on—ha! 'know all' Gadget Boy, and rrrsssppp!)

We bought some of the lemon drink, you could get clear or cream, we chose the clear yellow nectar. Pouring a glass when we retired, 'Cheers and bottoms up!' When our eyes had stopped watering and we could speak again, we croaked in unison, "You'd never guess it was strong eh?" We tried all sorts of mixers and didn't find anything that it was nice with, but it got drunk. We got the cream version the next time, and the next time . . .

We had twin beds and so slept well most of the time. At breakfast they did really good coffee. There was a selection of bread, cold meats and plastic cheese for breakfast! I partook of this Italian thing for the first breakfast, and had bread and jam for the rest of the week. We were hungry and it was raining, so we stopped at a restaurant. Waited a while then ordered lasagne, which came, after a while, and looked nice. "Is yours frozen?" he asked. Prodded into the middle to see, "Yes" it was. The waiter was called over who took both dishes away. After waiting fifteen minutes and having drunk our cappuccino, we left. Finding another restaurant with edible lasagne, and having a bottle of wine to celebrate.

A day trip to Naples started with a journey on the hydrofoil, which was at the bottom of a very steep, very curved hill. So much so that there were handrails and it also had a lot of steps. I did get to the bottom eventually, under instruction—"Bend your knees! Lean back! Swing your arms!" He had noticed and pointed out that I walk with my right arm tucked under my ribs. I am appalled and surprised that none of the physiotherapists I have seen have pointed this out to me. It's natural to swing your arms as you walk, it aids balance. He'd also previously pointed out that I walk with my big toes pointed up and that I stuck my bum out, as I walk very flat footed. He'd pointed it out; not the physiotherapists—who, one presumes, are trained and paid to point these obvious things out. Then they are trained to help you to correct these physical things, or try to (that's what it says in my dictionary).

We looked around the outside walls, wondering how high the moat had been filled with water, saying we'd come back now that we knew it was there. Had to kill more time with more cappuccino waiting for the hydrofoil. I'd never been on one of these before so I enjoyed the short expedition. There was a certain amount of time that we had to kill before the return to the hotel for dinner. We didn't really know where anything was and wandered around aimlessly, "Bend your knees, swing your arms." bitching about marquetry again. We'd been mooching around the shops a little while. This huge heavily tinselled chocolate egg caught my eye, so I bought it for my brother. Which meant carrying it around all day, good one, as Gadget Boy had all his photography equipment with him.

We stopped and had a pizza, a skinny biscuit with cheese your knife bounced off, then you had to wind round your fork to get in your mouth. Pizza was a one off; I thought it would be nice. We found this really interesting castle but hadn't enough time to go in to make it worthwhile to pay an entry fee.

The food at the hotel was very pretty and varied and you had bits of everything. It wasn't substantial enough, too airy fairy and clever—for my liking being a Yorkshire lass. When everything on your plate is doing something or pretending to be a flower (tomatoes, spring onions, radishes, carrots . . .)! You only get a little bit of the nice stuff too, they did lasagne once—as a starter. During the week there was a 'gala' night and the chef went berserk making birds out of butter, and cleverly disguising and distorting everything else that was edible. The waiters had put a strawberry in the middle of my desert as I was a 'pretty lady'. I was touched as the good looking waiter, doing our table, gave it to me. Ah . . .

They had live entertainment on the gala night. A couple were performing in the hotel bar. She was doing lead vocals and he was backing her, occasionally playing one of those keyboards that claps along too! She was wooing and warbling whilst shaking a green ball. In the non singing parts they were talking to some people out of our view. One couple got up and did the fox trot. We got up and left!

Being very adventurous we went by train to Herculane—a ruin excavated from volcanic mud, so it was unearthed pretty much intact. Amazing. I wonder if a Wimpy home would last so many years. It was weird 'walking' down streets and into houses that were bustling in 789 AD. It had been sunny when we set off. Lulled into a false sense of security I put some shorts on. I've brought them, I'm on holiday, and I'm wearing them! with the appropriate summery footwear. The passage underfoot was horrendous, it was a ruin, after a few hours my knees were beginning to ache so were my feet—sandals were not designed for hiking round ruins in the rain. There were paintings on the walls. The ones I did see were good, "Swing your arms, bend your knees, big toes down!" but I missed most as I was staring at the floor so I didn't fall and break one of my blue goose pimpled legs. I was freezing. On our way to a cafe to defrost I'd commented, "Everybody's gawping at me! the way I walk!" (being slightly paranoid now). "Everybody's gawping at you Gillian, as you are the only person in ITALY! who's wearing shorts!" But I was wearing a jumper and long jacket!

The mud sliding around the ruin meant the visit had to be cut short. Which I was not very happy about but as Gadget Boy said, "You did really well and we only missed a bit, that was probably the same as the rest, better to leave now!" I was still griping over coffee but he was right, for once. Gadget Boy took some photographs of my blue goose pimpled legs, and you can see how cold it was. Good job he had his camera with him! A warm bath had to be run the moment we returned to our room, the water hissed when I got in!

Another visit. A day trip to Pompeii to another ruin that dated around the same time as the excavation in Herculane. This town had been gassed by emissions from the volcano. It's situated right under Mount Vesuvious. They know this and were able to have made plaster casts of humans, by pouring plaster of Paris into the voids left after the bodies had decomposed. The one I remember was this chap who had been sitting down on the floor clutching his head and covering his eyes when he died. You could imagine the day.

There were lots of parties of school children, one group wore red baseball caps, another green, another wore yellow . . . What an excellent idea. Our tour guide told our group, "Just follow the umbrella!" Which one??! There were hundreds of groups and more umbrellas! But it was OK he could locate us, the blue plastic raincoats gang. Shaped blue carrier bags that we'd all had to buy, and wear. To make it obvious that we were stupid, optimistic tourists, as it was raining. The ground was a treacherous nightmare, and I didn't have sandals on this time. Nor shorts! In the 'red light' district of the ruin there were paintings on the walls and around windows, advertising what sexual positions were available on request. Everybody got a postcard showing one of these murals on which the woman had an abnormally huge bum and was on offer!

Onto the next stage of the trip, to get up Mount Vesuvious. Which would be extremely difficult I knew that, but I had support and therefore no doubt. "Swing your arms, lean into the mountain, bend . . ." Didn't listen to much more, I was concentrating on getting up a mountain without head butting it! DID IT !!!!!! (couldn't wait to tell you).

The coach took you up as far as it could and then you walked the rest of the way, getting back at four thirty—when the coach was leaving! We had paid a lot for the trip so were a bit annoyed when we had to pay again to get onto the mountain, which is why we were there! I still had no doubt that I could and would do this. What I didn't know was if it could be done in the allotted time and I didn't know how painful it would be. "Swing your arms, bend your knees, big toes down and lean into the mountain." Exactly, MOUNTAIN! I wasn't having a brilliant time but the view was amazing. Nearly there! and you had to pay again to get to the top, so near yet so far, you couldn't go all that way and NOT pay to complete the challenge! At the top we questioned if the steady emission of sulphur fumes meant anything.

Going back down was a COMPLETE NONSENSE, and hurt me a lot. With the constant jerky jarring motion on the descent, my feet, my knees and my diaphragm area were all causing me major distress. Looked at my watch, we were already late! My walking deteriorated. "Swing your arms, lean back, big . . ." "Fuck off!" I ordered keeping hold of his arm, we were "Already late!" I wailed. "They can't go without us, so swing your arms!" I didn't. The tour guide was walking towards us, a look of relief on his face. I apologised and explained that "Going up was hard, but coming down was too difficult!" Gadget Boy answered his confused look, "She was in a coma four years ago and she is disabled." He smiled, "Well done!" he said forgiving us for the hold up. I got on the coach first so that I could apologise to everybody. The rest of the party had all got back to the coach on time, and had been sitting for half an hour for their labours.

Stood at the front saying that I was sorry, that I wasn't too bad going up but coming down . . . and I shrugged and finished saying that I was, "Just sorry!" Even though I really was, I could not quell that YES!! feeling. It must have been obvious as I could hear the Germans at the front growling. They didn't look too pretty either! At the back near to where we where seated an English man grinned at me, "You did it!!!"

Words of congratulating approval from the English crowd. I wrote this achievement on all my big bums (the postcards). Gadget Boy bought me a big chunky necklace made with polished pieces of rock-lava, to wear instead of the one I had on. I liked the necklace I had on, it just so happens that Pathetic bought it for me. But that wasn't the reason I liked it, I explained, I just . . . did! He obviously didn't.

Still not too happy that we had had to pay out so many times extra to the original fee, and weren't warned about it, I told Gadget Boy that I was going to tell the 'rep' when we got back! We might not have had any spare money after paying extra to get into the Pompeii ruin. Meaning nothing to eat! or drink! Using exaggeration to effect, or not. "But we didn't, and I've got plenty of money, so you'd be lying!" he stated. "That isn't my point!" I argued with venom; "I haven't and neither will some others." repeating that we should have been told. That's what holiday reps are for! Warning him that if he repeated this in front of her, making me look, "A complete idiot!" I'd punch him.

He went up to the room. I went to locate the rep on duty that night. Whilst I was saying my piece a man with a stick came up, he was very upset and eager to say his. So I rounded mine off, she was getting on my nerves any way. She kept saying, "With all due respect!" every other sentence and it was already obvious she couldn't really give a toss and wasn't really listening. With all due respect. This man had been to Pompeii too, and had been totally thrown off course with the cobbled, different levelled, very uneven surface. So much so that his, also elderly, wife had almost had a heart attack having to almost carry him. "And was beside myself with worry all day!!!" she added. Yes! she should have warned us about that too!, I'd forgotten about that (he didn't do Mount Vesuvius). "Well, you've had your wrists severely slapped tonight haven't you?" I laughed trying to make light. "That's nothing new!" She turned away from me, so I didn't know whether or not that was funny? I left to go and argue about parquetry or something.

Saw the same man later that evening at the hotel bar where he told us that he'd just had to call the hotel staff to get him out of the bath. He was, "Stuck, again!" But not only in this hotel, he explained. He'd been stuck in baths, "All over the world!" Laughing we asked him 'why did he keep getting in?' He never thought he'd get stuck, until he did! Fair enough, if I knew when I was going to fall over I'd never get up! Gadget Boy asked me what I wanted to drink? "Don't know—surprise me!" I had said, to be presented with an all singing and dancing holiday cocktail.

Another day trip that started on a ferry. A gorgeously sunny day and a very scenic trek to Capri—'Millionaire's Island'. Well what a disappointment. All that we saw was the touristy bit, where you were spoilt for choice with T-shirts. Cable car up to another spot on the island—where you got a choice of more expensive shirts. "Swing your arms, bend your knees . . ." We went into an hotel to pick up their brochure to look up the prices of staying there. They must have gold leaf sheets! We had been told that you have to sell your kids to get a coffee! We hadn't any kids between us but we had 'no worries', as he had plenty of money, or I could sell him! No, maybe not.

On the ferry ride back it was cold, wet and windy. The sea windswept and choppy. There was a couple seated, who had been 'lulled' this morning and were wearing shorts. They looked very fed up and were shivering and turning blue visibly. Now ask me if I felt ever so smug in my JEANS? I went better than that, slowly pulling a sweater AND a jacket from my rucksack. Should we put the umbrella up too as we'd got one? We had bought it whilst on the trip to Herculane, when I'd worn shorts, and it was covered in cappuccino. Opening it I'd swiped the frothy top off his coffee, then dripped it all over his head (note head not hair).

We were told about a bar that had live music, and it was just round the corner from the hotel. So the glad rags went on and we went out to investigate. We were the only people in there other than the band, we were the audience—all two of us. We clapped very loud sarcastically whilst looking around after the first song. They laughed, they were very good and nice. We chatted to them between songs, once or twice to ask who did the original to what they had just sung. You know when you can see the person in your head but just cannot remember their names? Isn't it annoying? Well I'll tell you what's more annoying, when people come up to you smiling and greet you by name. Then ask about your brother and parents, and you haven't got a clue who they are. At first you just grin foolishly thinking 'I'll remember who they are in a minute!', then they're gone! I'm a bit quicker to say something now, before I got known as 'that woman who just grins vacantly'.

It was the last night and I was all dressed for a night at the piano bar. Gadget Boy sat next to me on the bed, he'd been ages in the bathroom so I'd got a drink. Oh . . . oh! he looked very pensive. "Gillian . . . I want to talk about our relationship. What do you feel about me?" I took my shoes off and poured myself another drink. He went on, "I don't think we get on very well . . . do we?" Maybe arguing about marquetry and such like, every day, was a bit of an indication. I couldn't answer, what else was there to say? He asked me again what I thought of him? I tried to answer that him being my physiotherapist all day was irritating and the role reversal with no slushy thoughtful bits was hurtful, disappointing and confusing.

Tolerance was a fitting word, and he REALLY should know why. I don't like getting about like this and being told it's abnormal, and looks so. ALL day everyday. With the under current that if it was you . . . you cannot imagine how you would feel, and what you would still be capable of. I'm ever aware of how close I was to never walking again, having a catheter forever, not being able to speak or doing anything else, ever again. Then what do you do with what's left? It's not an identifiable enigma, one gets distracted by easy options that aren't so easy for me any more. That's not abnormal.

It's tiresome, moreso when you want to look around and be in a new different country with a special person. This was the point at which I really reacted and answered him. He told me what he thought of me, I saw him 'as a meal ticket'. My first thought was 'conceited git', but what I stammered was: "Whoa . . . hang on, you invited me to come with you and you paid, as you have, 'lots of money' and I haven't." The answer was a little terse as it was true. But I had my own money, I'd brought with me what I could handle. I reminded him of a few times that I'd volunteered to pay for lunch, and he'd stopped me. I'd paid my own way on all the excursions the trains and ferries etc . . . entries and fares. We argued all night and finished off the lemon drink. Went to sleep stinking drunk, with a stinking mood on, an excellent last night. When you huff really loudly and poignantly pull every bit of your torso, bit by bit, as far away from theirs as possible. A bit pointless in twin beds, but still!

I was awake first the next morning and finished packing my case as we were leaving in a few hours. I wasn't being noisy on purpose but neither was I trying to be quiet. He stirred, I remembered last night and was momentarily irritated, "You WANKER!" was his wake up call. He accused me of crashing and banging on purpose to wake him up. Oh please, if I'd really wanted to wake him up, a glass of cold water would have been used, and anyway, "I didn't want to wake you up!" I finished packing. I asked for my drugs that he'd been safe guarding, he threw them at me.

Whilst attempting to pack breakable gifts carefully in my nylon suitcase I knocked one of my fancy bottles onto the floor, scattering the contents irretrievably. "That's one down already." I commented. So they were packed in his suitcase that had been made for transporting pretend pottery plates, lemon glasses and chocolate eggs overseas. I closed my suitcase and defiantly lugged it to the door to take it downstairs. He was still in bed.

Stumbling jerkily every step of the way, and banging into everything. Getting temporarily stuck in the lift with my suitcase jammed in the doorway, which meant that everybody in the foyer was now looking at me. I dragged the suitcase, thankfully free of breakable gifts, across the foyer to join the other suitcases, awaiting transport to the airport. "Gatwick?" I was asked, "No, Manchester." I replied. The Gatwick flight was now and my flight was at five that afternoon but he would take my case for the day. I burst into tears. A whole day left in Italy, with that idiot! It was raining and I was quite pleased about this. Now I could tell people, with all honesty that it rained, "EVERY day!" It was grey. Went back upstairs to break the good news that we'd got a whole day left in Italy, together. It said the departure times on the tickets, that he'd got, but he'd got it wrong. Very wrong but, he, "Didn't really need glasses!"

Outside the hotel he grabbed my hand, grinning sheepishly, and squeezed it. How our relationship started and ended. We had the best day of the week, well I did. I'm cross with myself whilst I'm writing this, in that I fell for the 'sorry little boy' act, I should have broken his fingers, so he couldn't be a wanker anymore.

He asked how much money I had left. Enough for some duty free cigarettes, some fresh lemons that we'd seen in the market—complete with the branch, the leaves and the flowers—for my mum, another replacement bottle of that lemon drink for my dad . . . I got the cash out of my pocket to check I'd got enough for these things. "You've got too much—way too much!" Gadget Boy's eyes bounced out of his head, so they could see better. Don't worry I'll spend what I have left I assured him. I bought some lemon chocolate that looked nice and wasn't, my brother liked the leftovers. The stall selling the bottles of spices had sold out of the replacement I wanted, I chuntered to Gadget Boy about the broken bottle and how annoyed I still was with him! "Hang on . . ." he said, "You broke it!" Pause, "Oh yeah!"; I'd forgotten.

Apparently, I "Do that all the time!" Yes, I forget things all the time, an annoying consequence of having been in a coma, I reminded him. What I don't do all the time is agree with you, telling you how 'state of the art' your toys are, whilst telling you that I'm eternally grateful that you have expendable funds and I don't!!

He had gifts to buy too. I can't recall him buying anything that said 'Italy' for anybody except his ex girlfriend's daughter. The ex of five years, "Who desperately wants me back." whose sixteen year old daughter, "Still needs" and still, "Misses and cries" for him. I can imagine! He bought her a bracelet made with lumps of polished rock, lava. It was actually very nice and I said that the necklace, that he'd bought for me, would "Go nicely."

The walk to the other terminal to collect the car, was long and not needed. I was very tired and walking was becoming painful and I was acting accordingly. "Is it much further?" I kept asking. The reply "See . . . I told you it was a long way!" explained the dodgy start to the holiday and didn't do much to appease me. When we returned home he warned me, "I have to go and see her!" "Why do you 'have to'?" I'd asked. "Because I want to!!" he'd snapped. "Oh." He told me later on the phone that, "She said that she loved the necklace and bracelet!"

He took millions of photographs, using lots of different techniques, and mine were better I thought! The photographs I took were simple and straightforward, my camera wouldn't do anything else! Remember I had bought a new set of posh clothing for the wedding and I got dressed up when we went out in the evening in Italy. Space Girl, looking at the pictures, asked "Did you wear the same thing every day?" On every photo I'm wearing my brown jeans, look hungover, fat and old! Except on the snaps of my blue legs. He didn't take one picture of me looking nice, as in smartly dressed. I lie, he took one photo of me at the wedding— I'm seated with some of his family, and you can see that I'm holding a cigarette and most of my forehead. My hair looks good though! He wasn't taking the photo of me obviously, I just happened to be there. In the way. If he'd wanted the photo of just me, he could have done that by 'gadgeting' with his big and clever toy (that isn't a double entente/ entendre? Something like that).

HAIRY CHEST—FINALE

They're happy, got their gadgets,
Can afford to play and be a control freak,
Satisfied in gadget world with no real need to venture.
Don't interrupt, don't disagree don't get in the way,
". . . only because I want you to get better . . . swing your arms . . ."
A commitment that has no buttons or dials!?
Doesn't respond normally!?
Must be broken! Throw it away.
Can buy a new one.

CHAPTER THIRTEEN

'd brought back some pasta that was three foot long, Erm . . . lots of centimetres, for Teeny, who asked for, "A pizza!" It came back safely as it fit in his case, with everything else. My case was just full of clean summer clothes. When I gave it to her, with a whole jar of spices, I asked if I could break a piece of the pasta to see how fragile it was. Could I break it? She'll have to smash it with a hammer to fit it into a saucepan, and then it will take hours to cook. Looks good though.

The egg for my brother was on my floor at legs length, being a football, for weeks. When he took the foil off, the chocolate egg was not covered or boxed or broken. It could have gone in my cheap suitcase too! It was like a giant Kinder Surprise, as there was something in the middle. A set of four linked photograph frames in pink and green foamy plastic, very Italian! "To put photographs of your kids in!" I joked as his girlfriend had been telling me how broody she felt. He laughed, but not a lot. He went leaving behind his egg and loads of other rubbish, he ALWAYS leaves loads of junk when he visits. It drives me MAD!, is it to remind me he's been? bless! He used to always cut his toe-nails on my floor, until I threatened to save them all up to, "Season his food with, one day! But you won't know when!"

Dad had the bird and I telephoned him when we got back. Remembering to ask about the bird just before the receiver was replaced. "He . . . is . . . very . . . messy!" he tutted, "Isn't he!" I agreed.

A few days after we returned there were those mud slides in Naples that killed people who could run away.

Gadget Boy read this account of 'Italy' and sat sniggering when he'd finished. Gosh! My ego was smashed when I discovered it wasn't due to my writing. "You're gonna' love this!" he confided. He'd bought a radio that tunes into radio stations worldwide. Excellent gadget, I agreed and then asked if he understood any of them?

A lady that I know had to have two separate mastectomies. She was telling me of a friend of hers that had said, with little thought, "Don't worry, just think of what you still have." People have said that to me. "DON'T think, or talk, about the horrid bits and what you have lost! Think of what you still have!" When you're trying to stay calm and say through gritted teeth, "That wasn't the point!" Isn't it exasperating when this goes on?

If it's happening to you it's very natural to think about the shitty side to such things, what could this mean? It's weird to dwell in morbid thought, until the worst scenario is a reality. None of us want to be different, we all want to 'fit'. As a race we are incredibly cruel to those who don't, survival of the fittest? Fat kids at school, kids with braces, the huge Mount Vesuvius (climbed it) zit that's appeared—unknown to you, until you get home—right in the middle of your face, the really funny looking guy with the huge penis shaped nose, those that walk funny as though they're alcoholics . . . Well I know that I'm not so sure that I am overjoyed with standing out, for whatever reason but the most obvious does spring to mind. The runt left behind struggling to survive against all the odds.

Walking around where I live, with Space Girl, there are always new bits I haven't seen. I don't wander so far on my own, I lack the confidence, skill and motivation. Oh yeah and the memory to get back, but that's alright at the moment as I'm a novelist/writer! But (hopefully?), this will be finished soon. Then what will I do?

We found a shop, in a back street, that sells delicatessen food stuffs and oils. They hadn't got walnut oil which I had been introduced to in Italy, it was used as a salad dressing. It is so nice that I am going to buy four bottles, one for me, my mum, my dad and my brother. Space Girl has left and I can't remember where the shop is, the shop owner is getting some oil in for me as well. But I will be seeing Space Girl in a few weeks. We're going to see Macbeth at an open air theatre—I've got the cappuccino stained brolly that Gadget Boy didn't need, living in a desert—and I'll forget to ask her. So when she reads this, "Where is that shop?"

(The outdoor MacBeth venture, 'pear shaped'. Space Girl called on the day and it was decided that sitting outside all night in the rain wasn't really a fun thing and neither of us had read this work. So I still don't know where the walnut oil shop is).

We found a tattoo studio; Space Girl has got a trendy tattoo (that she fainted for!) to be part of a gang of girls going on holiday. Spruce Girl also had one done to go to Cyprus, Teeny has got two. I wanted to go in. There were two men in there and I started chatting almost straight away. One of them was having a tattoo and had a few already, and it 'took hours' to choose those too! Looking around the room, covered with options of various colour size and detail, I was not surprised. But I was surprised at some of the designs, did people really have some of these pictures etched onto their bodies forever? Do modern tattoos turn into a faded green smudge with age? Pathetic has one such mess on one of his arms, I don't know what it was but it looks like a condom was drawn now.

I told the tattoo shop men my latest joke:

A man is shipwrecked on an island with a dog and a pig, after a few months he starts to really fancy the pig. Approaches it, 'sweetie', and the dog attacks him. Tries again and the dog bites him, has one more go and the dog gets him.

A woman is shipwrecked and the man saves her life, she is so grateful that she swears to do anything! in gratitude. "What, anything?" the man asks. "Absolutely!" is the reply. "Can you take the dog for a walk?" the man asks. (My dad told me this on the phone, "Are you writing it down?" he kept asking, is that OK)?

One of the men, smiling, said, "Are you pissed?" Snorted with indifference and turned to Space Girl asking if she heard that and repeating what he'd said. Turning back I answered "No, I'm disabled." No, no he meant because I was telling jokes "an' everythin'!" He was rather cute, I watched him having some of his tattoo done—right that's enough of that and I still don't want one, we left. It's a good job I don't, I haven't got a clue where this shop is either.

In the writing class 'homework' I always (when I do it) manage to tie it in with the book. I can't remember the title to this but I do know that it would have had a very weak link.

"I am here my friends, to tell you there is hope . . ." a starting point for a writing exercise, chosen from a selection given:

. . . well, look at me . . .

From coma, to this—a time that words cannot explain enough. They cannot fully describe the complete trauma and frustrations. You couldn't comprehend anyway unless, you were 'there'. A time for lots of questions to lots of medical 'experts' with lots of varied answers . . . my family and I were soon to realize that nobody knows.

We all have theories, and I think I know what my hardships/problems are. Well I'd be a bit of an ignorant bag if I didn't! I meet me every day. So, I won't be told, I won't be given vague textbook blanketed theories any more—they bore me.

Scoring highly on popularity scales again I'm sure. Who knows? Me—I know me.

POEMAY

What to do instead?
Think quick before you're dead.
Nothing stops the clocks,
They tick and we're in a box,
To join the wandering stars,
Maybe ending up on Mars.
One thing for sure everyone dies.
Look deep into my eyes,
An inviting vacuous cave,
Destined for the grave.
Could go surfing in the sea!
SELF DENIAL! . . . again,
Could be good!
I'll be heartbroken swimming like a brick again . . .
What to do instead?

Think of a word ending that you like, now think of ten words that end in this way. Then in the confinement of four sentences use these words. You should try this, it's a challenge:

Life is full of tension, in my opinion, and don't mention education. Trying to fulfil the second life given to me takes some exertion, what a commotion. The notion being that one is out and about, in action, and meeting people. The exercise on alliteration causes a rift in the ocean's motion—completion should of course bring elation

Looking out of a window onto a busy crossroads and a bustle of sometimes high buildings, observing with an open mind. What I was seeing was busy, fast, moving, self involved, we are 'drops in the ocean'. But at the end of that day we are all part of our own families and have a life. Then going with this flow I thought, we are striving continually to better ourselves and to broaden our horizons, everywhere on almost everything. Then that begs the questions have we gone as far as we can? Do we want/

need to go any further? What will the reaction be to all our actions? We already know that the ozone layer, that surrounds and protects our planet, is being depleted/destroyed by us living the way that we do. Just maybe we are not the centre of the universe and we are being looked down on by someone who's sucking in breath . . . 'there goes another one that got too greedy'. We know what elements attack the defense of this sheath. When we destroy it completely.

The conclusion to this ego trip is, that I can write in 'different' styles—but I can only write about one thing, me. Sad, but I must be interesting—or obsessed.

On this writing course a woman that I had met, and known for two days wrote a poem. She gave it to me to read and on completion I said, "This could have been written for me . . ."

"It was." she replied:

Monopoly—no Victory. For Gillian—with hope.

Some lives straightforward sequence,
All four sides, complete the square.
Collecting their two hundred pounds
They pass "GO" every time
Rarities though,
And pattern creates its own problems!
Because our first life didn't complete the square,
A new life has been given us,
The plan is different:
With adapted apparatus,
It plays by different rules.
The bird with one wing is grounded now
And can't soar over the golden cornfields.
Someone must throw grain for it
On it's own little patch of ground.

Oh, wounded one.
Other birds may be kept for show,
Beauty, strength or pride, flight and prowess;
But you are kept
Only for your dear self;
Wounded, 'useless', loved,
And someday, even you will know it.

F. Mary Callan

CHAPTER FOURTEEN

My case manager was visiting and Spruce Girl was making coffee using my best cups and saucers for them and giving me a goldfish bowl. My everyday cups are big. Chatting away and the conversation turned to bosom and bras My case manager was asking Spruce Girl what kind of bra she wore, and telling us what kind she wore. Still talking boobs, "They are very firm." and she got them out to prove a point. They looked firm! and big! Spruce Girl joined in and got hers out! hers are big too! Wanting to be a part of this floorshow on my floor! I got mine out as well. Conversation stood still momentarily. Reminding me of the time when I was younger and developing, I was telling my mum that, "I need a bra!" My aunty happened to be there and, boosting my little ego, observed "Gillian . . . you need corn plasters!" ha ha. I bet I just wet myself. Well compared with these two today, both double Gs! I hadn't graduated much. I put mine away, which wasn't difficult.

Just to update you about Bird. From having no tail and being smacked with his cage that time that he wouldn't come out of my bedroom at bedtime. Now I open his cage door in the morning when he is uncovered, and he just flies around everywhere all day. As free as a . . . then at night he's in his cage and I cover him. Excellent, it's either take yourself or get bashed again. He's standing on my head right now—he still won't let me touch him though. Tart! AND I let him crap all over everything!

I have decided that this 'autobiography' will finish (that is, being recorded and added to—not writing it) at the end of May. It's poetic and apt. It will be four years exactly since the accident. I honestly think that I've made just about all the improvements that I will—on a major scale. It's just refining what I have left now. The comparison from now to four years ago . . . there is none. From being able to do nothing for myself, even breathing, to what I am achieving now. The wheelchair went ages ago, although it was still with me when I moved into the flat. It was taken for somebody who needed it(!). It was weird letting it go, it had been an essential part of my life for a long time. Exhilarated but afraid. I didn't feel quite the same when the hydraulic bath chair went, it was a pain, (and it's incredibly long to type!).

So here we are, four years after impact. A frustrating and painful fall into the unknown, out of the black void into another one. You just never know . . . Along the way there have been a lot of people that have made a difference in my life, welcome and otherwise. But what do I think? I think that some people should just shut up and crawl away, but I have never been a very patient person by all accounts, an aptitude exaggerated by my head injury, so that I have none now. When I was at the Unit a member of staff in her authoritarian voice instructed me that "Patience is a virtue." My reply is still, "I'm sure it is . . . if you can wait long enough. Then you die."

An attitude that has endeared and made friendships, so that I have none now.

If we have food mountains in some parts of the world why are people starving to death in others? If we have unemployed doctors and nurses why are people dying needlessly? Why are we suffering the effects of cutbacks within the public sector when it costs thousands of pounds per year to keep murderers in prison for life? Why are children killing each other? How do adults get any pleasure from messing sexually with children? or animals? If we put animals asleep to stop pain and suffering, of our beloved family pets, why do we make confirmed terminally ill people go on suffering physical and mental pain until the sad inevitable end? Making the families suffer too? We are such a caring thoughtful society and should therefore make euthanasia a legal choice. Why are nuclear arms still being tested? What, to see if they still work? When all the fish in the world are luminous green with beards will that convince us?

I'm getting on my soapbox a bit here aren't I? and wandering so far from the initial point that I have no idea what I was talking about. Oh yeah . . . I was trying to conclude this ego trip.

So before I go I'll tell you of the most amazing thing in all of this. Right at the beginning when I had just surfaced from the coma and was still in intensive care. The cleaner told my mum, "She be OK . . . just a leedle thing wrong . . . she maybe be blind in one eye."

Well waddya know?

My last, and newest joke:

> There are three bits of tarmac in the bar having a drink This big piece of black tarmac comes in. Ooer! who's he? The barman asks.
> I'm the M4 and I'm well 'ard! So watch it! Who are you?
> We're just pavement your motorway ship! Then a big piece of pink tarmac comes in and the bits of pavement run away?
> Who's this geezer? the M4 asks the bar man. Who sucks in breath and shakes his head, Ah man you've got to watch out for him . . . he's a cycle path!

Anyway, this is important and it's my book! So there . . . actions speak louder but,

XXX THANK YOU MOM XXXX—smak!!

XXX THANK YOU PAND XXXX—smak!!

XXX THANK YOU DAD XXXX—smak!!

Gadget Boy—ta mate!
'ED'—more than words can say!

That's it, enough said . . . seeya.

Headway Coventry & Warwickshire

'TRAGIC, DISTURBING, UPLIFTING, HUMOROUS, SAD, MANY, HOPEFUL, LAPHTERS, ... Her told Go without CAN'T WAIT FOR SEQUEL II'

Give me something honest down to earth such as yours everytime.

I just thought I would like to write and say how much your book is being appreciated to the point where I now need two more copies.

From the account of making a packet lemon meringue cheesecake to illegal vodka in her knicker drawer. Gillian's sense of humour serves her

Congratulations Gillian

Your book is a triumph!

Your vigorous style makes for compelling reading - I started and certainly put it down.

epilepsy action

This extraordinary book was written by Gillian Firth 'Mark Two': witty, wry, chatty and very, coma. Gillian tells her story in her own inimitable way: very honest.

HEADW... 'GSTOKE

Sense & Humour 10

Thank you for writing the book, will there be another one?

Enjoying the book please send another

people have asked me to get for them. I would like to order two copies of your book which

Well what can I say....I think the book was EXCELLENT. AMAZING ! THOUGHT PROVOKING, FUNNY & SAD. OK, your head is big enough now !!! Seriously, once I started reading it I just didn't want to put it down.

I have just finished reading your book. Decompelling reading of what!! It is brilliant full of confidence

I have started to read it today. I love your attitude. I've had a few Pathetics.

I read you book and thought it was brilliant

well. A thought provoking book and an inspiration for anyone recovering from, or caring for, a head injury survivor.

Your book made me laugh and cry and it most certainly only made me think. I loved the book.

Headway
Basingstoke

...was compulsive reading I can't begin to imagine the amount of work that went into it, an excellent endeavour.

'loved the code names

published this book yourself? ...tery are your the most determined person.

Cover is really good

I am ordering two copies of your book

really as enjoying your book. he two copies
we xmas presents.
for two boo

I *think* I am sorry to trouble you again but need another two copies of book. This is really because the last one was going around the Rehabilitatic Unit in Plymouth and so many people were interested in it that I had to leave my copies there!

Thankyou, thankyou..... for putting your story into print. Oh, how everyone should read it it gives such an insight into the devastating and lasting effects of a serious brain injury.

This book tracks her life in the four years following her accident

(I like the nicknames you've given people

style is intimate and fresh

I have also recovered from a Traumatic Brain Injury

I liked the "warts and all" approach.

I devoured it in two days
since then have found myself thinking
of it almost constantly.

I have only just started
amusing and witty and so

with your amazing life story.

very readable. What an interesting life you have led.

FIND THE BOOK REALLY FUNNY

HEADWAY BEDFORD

P.O. Box 01,
Selby (0
N.York's
Y08-8YJ
£9.99 £2.01 P+P.

www.ingramcontent.com/pod-product-compliance
Lightning Source LLC
Chambersburg PA
CBHW021625120626
46545CB00002B/407